Alabama's

Forests, 2005

Andrew J. Hartsell and
Tony G. Johnson

United States
Department of
Agriculture

Forest Service

Southern
Research Station

Resource Bulletin
SRS-146

Andrew J. Hartsell is a Research Forester with the U.S. Department of Agriculture Forest Service, Southern Research Station, Forest Inventory and Analysis Research Work Unit, Knoxville, TN 37919.

Tony G. Johnson is a Resource Analyst with the U.S. Department of Agriculture Forest Service, Southern Research Station, Forest Inventory and Analysis Research Work Unit, Knoxville, TN 37919.

Front cover: top left, sweetgum and yellow-poplar are two of the more abundant hardwood species in Alabama. (photo courtesy of the Alabama Forestry Commission); top right, mixed pine/hardwood forest in Colbert County. (photo by Kelvin J. Daniels); bottom, sawtooth oak in Marshall County. (photo by Kelvin J. Daniels). Back cover: top left, daybreak in a hardwood forest. (photo by L. David Dwinell); top right, sweetgum and yellow-poplar. (photo courtesy of the Alabama Forestry Commission); bottom, stream in Colbert County. (photo by Kelvin J. Daniels).

Leaves of a red maple. (photo by Andrew J. Hartsell)

Alabama's

Forests, 2005

Andrew J. Hartsell and Tony G. Johnson

Waterfall in Colbert County.
(photo by Kelvin J. Daniels)

Linda Casey

Jimmy L. Reaves

The Great State of Alabama celebrates a rich history rooted in its natural environment and diverse and productive forest resources. The citizens of Alabama receive multiple benefits from these extensive resources (now referred to as "ecosystem services"), including timber and nontimber forest products, recreation opportunities (e.g., hiking, hunting, and camping), and clean air and water. To adequately protect and monitor forest resource quantity and quality and recognizing the need for information documenting changes taking place in our forests, it is important to have the means for assessing the extent and condition of our forest resources. Since the 1930s, the U.S. Forest Service has provided the means through the Forest Inventory and Analysis (FIA) program, which conducts inventories of public and private land, nationwide, on regular time intervals. We appreciate the cooperation of other public agencies and private landowners in providing access to measurement plots.

Over the last 11 years, FIA has approached this inventory through a working partnership between the Alabama Forestry Commission and the Forest Service Southern Research Station's FIA program, which has strengthened and improved Alabama's forest inventory. The quality of this report is a direct result of that sustained cooperation.

This report contains information on the forest resources of Alabama that will be used by industry decisionmakers, foresters, students, and researchers involved in forestry and forestry-related fields. Recognizing that forest resources include much more than volume and numbers of trees alone, this report includes information on forest health, ecological values, and an evaluation of the goals and objectives of Alabama forest landowners.

It is with great pride that we present this information on the forests of Alabama. It is our goal that the partnership and cooperative nature of this effort between our two organizations will continue to deliver the best information on the forests of Alabama now and in the future.

Linda Casey
Linda Casey
Alabama State Forester,
Alabama Forestry Commission

Jimmy L. Reaves
Director, Southern Research Station,
Forest Service

Foreword

This bulletin highlights the principal findings of the eighth forest survey of Alabama. Field work began in January 2001 and was completed in December 2005. Seven previous surveys, completed in 1936, 1953, 1963, 1972, 1982, 1990, and 2000, provide data that researchers can use to measure changes and trends over the past 64 years. This bulletin primarily emphasizes changes and trends since 1972.

Periodic surveys of forest resources are authorized by the Forest and Rangeland Renewable Resources Research Act of 1978. These surveys are a continuing, nationwide undertaking by the regional experiment stations of the Forest Service, U.S. Department of Agriculture. Inventories of the 13 Southern States (Alabama, Arkansas, Florida, Georgia, Kentucky, Louisiana, Mississippi, North Carolina, Oklahoma, South Carolina, Tennessee, Texas, and Virginia) and the Commonwealth of Puerto Rico are conducted by the Southern Research Station (SRS), Forest Inventory and Analysis (FIA) Research Work Unit, operating from its headquarters in Knoxville, TN, and offices in Asheville, NC, and Starkville, MS. The primary objective of these surveys is to periodically inventory and evaluate all forest and related resources. These multiresource data help provide a basis for formulating forest policies and programs and for the orderly development and use of the resources. This bulletin discusses the extent and condition of forest land; associated timber volumes; and rates of timber growth, mortality, and removals.

Tabular data included in FIA reports are designed to provide a comprehensive array of forest resource statistics, but additional data can be obtained for those who require more specialized information. The forest resource data for Southern States can be accessed directly via the Internet at http://srsfia2.fs.fed.us/. Data in a format common to the two FIA units in the Eastern United States are also available. These data may be obtained from the Internet site referenced above.

Additional information about any aspect of this survey may be obtained from:

Forest Inventory and Analysis
Research Work Unit
U.S. Department of Agriculture
Forest Service
Southern Research Station
4700 Old Kingston Pike
Knoxville, TN 37919
Telephone: 865-862-2000
William G. Burkman
Program Manager

Acknowledgments

The SRS gratefully acknowledges the cooperation and invaluable assistance provided by the Alabama Forestry Commission (AFC) in the collection of field data. This bulletin was made possible through the collaboration of the Forest Service FIA personnel (including those in Data Collection, Information Management, Analysis, and Publication Management). We also appreciate the cooperation of other public agencies and private landowners in providing access to measurement plots.

The author thanks James F. Rosson, Jr., and Anita K. Rose, who contributed their time and knowledge in the areas of sampling and statistics (Rosson) and forest health (Rose). Their reviews, edits, and commentary were extremely helpful. All data and tables pertaining to down woody material and ozone damage were compiled by Anita Rose. Brian Hendricks, State Coordinator of the AFC, provided information about the State's forest resources and managed the State field crews.

Contents

Effects of southern pine beetle on a loblolly stand. (photo by L. David Dwinell)

Contents

Bottlebrush buckeye.
(photo by David
Stephens, Bugwood.org)

List of Figures

Eastern tiger swallowtail butterfly. (photo by Andrew J. Hartsell)

Page

Hardwood forest. (photo courtesy of the Alabama Forestry Commission)

Stream in Colbert County. (photo by Kelvin J. Daniels)

Mixed pine/hardwood forest in Colbert County. (photo by Kelvin J. Daniels)

Area

• Alabama lost 298,000 acres (1.3 percent) of its forest land between the 2000 and 2005 inventories. Alabama gained 3.8 million acres of forest land between the 1936 and 2005 inventories.

• One-fourth (6.3 million acres) of Alabama's forest land was in plantations at the time of the 2005 inventory.

Ownership

• Family forests accounted for 15.3 million acres (67 percent) of the State's forest land at the time of the 2005 inventory.

• At the time of the 2005 inventory, owners of more than one-half of Alabama's family forest acreage reported that some form of timber harvesting had taken place on their lands within the previous 5 years.

Volume

• At the time of the 2005 inventory, Alabama's total growing-stock volume was 28.3 billion cubic feet, up from 11.7 billion cubic feet since the 1953 inventory.

• At the time of the 2005 inventory, total all-live volume was up 6.9 percent for softwoods and 1.2 percent for hardwoods since the 2000 inventory.

• Loblolly pine accounted for 72 percent of the State's softwood volume at the time of the 2005 inventory.

• The increase in loblolly pine volume between the 2000 and 2005 inventories exceeded the 2005 inventory volume of any other softwood species in the State.

• At the time of the 2005 inventory, other red oaks was the most prevalent hardwood species group statewide, representing 4.1 million cubic feet of all-live volume.

Growth, Removals, and Mortality

• Softwood growing-stock growth averaged 995.2 million cubic feet per year over the period 2000–2005. Growing-stock growth exceeded removals, which averaged 827.4 million cubic feet per year, for the first time since the 1972 inventory.

• Hardwood growing-stock growth averaged 517 million cubic feet per year over the period 2000–2005 and exceeded removals, which averaged 394 million cubic feet per year.

Plantations

• Plantations accounted for 40 percent of the State's all-live softwood volume, and are responsible for a majority of Alabama's average annual softwood growth and removals, 67 and 55 percent, respectively.

• Less than 3 percent of the all-live hardwood volume is in plantations.

• Seventy-five percent of the all-live softwood volume in planted stands exists in the 6-, 8-, and 10-inch diameter classes, combined.

A managed pine stand. (photo courtesy of the Alabama Forestry Commission)

Forest Health

• Average annual mortality of all-live trees in Alabama, for both hardwood and softwood species, has increased with each inventory from 1990 through 2005.

• The 2005 inventory was the first in which mortality of softwoods exceeded mortality of hardwoods. Softwood losses due to insects (up more than 200 percent since the last survey) were the primary driver for this increase.

• Tree mortality averaged 219 million cubic feet of all-live softwoods and 198 million cubic feet of hardwoods per year during the period of the 2005 inventory.

• Down woody material in Alabama forests averaged 11.7 tons per acre at the time of the 2005 inventory.

• Ozone damage was found at only 2.3 percent of the ozone biomonitoring sites in Alabama. The Southwide average was 20.6 percent of sites.

Timber Products and the Economic Impact

• There were about 145 primary wood-processing plants in Alabama in 2005. These plants employed more than 33,000 individuals and had an annual payroll of nearly $1.33 billion.

• Between 2000 and 2005, the State's output of timber products averaged 1.32 billion cubic feet per year. Roundwood products accounted for 86 percent of this total and mill byproducts the rest.

• Pulpwood and saw logs were the roundwood products produced in greatest quantity between 2000 and 2005. Pulpwood production totaled nearly 681 million cubic feet in 2005, while saw-log production totaled almost 416 million cubic feet. These two items accounted for 83 percent of total product output in 2005.

A hardwood drain provides the water necessary for a diverse understory. (photo by Andrew J. Hartsell)

A stream in Colbert County. (photo by Kelvin J. Daniels)

This bulletin presents the findings of the eighth survey of Alabama's forest resources (fig. 1). Earlier inventories have been performed by the Forest Service, Southern Forest Experiment Station. The first of these was performed in 1936 (Duerr 1946). This was followed up by surveys performed in 1953 (Wheeler 1953), 1963 (Sternitzke 1963), 1972 (Murphy 1973), 1982 (Rudis 1984), and 1990 (McWilliams 1992). In 1995 the Southern Forest Experiment Station, headquartered in New Orleans, LA, merged with the Southeastern Forest Experiment Station, headquartered in Asheville, NC, to become the Southern Research Station (SRS,) which is headquartered in Asheville, NC. A seventh inventory of Alabama's forests was conducted by the SRS Forest Inventory and Analysis (FIA) in 2000 (Hartsell 2009) in conjunction with the Alabama Forestry

Commission (AFC). The AFC performed the majority of the field work, and SRS personnel provided oversight. SRS is responsible for processing, disseminating, and reporting the data.

Initial surveys of the South's forest resources centered on the availability of timber for harvest. During this period, the specter of a timber famine or shortage of wood was a primary concern. Commercial timber remained the focus of FIA surveys until the 1980s. Therefore, earlier publications reported on volume, growth, removals, and mortality of growing stock on timberland.

Trumpet pitcher plants.
(photo by Bill Lea)

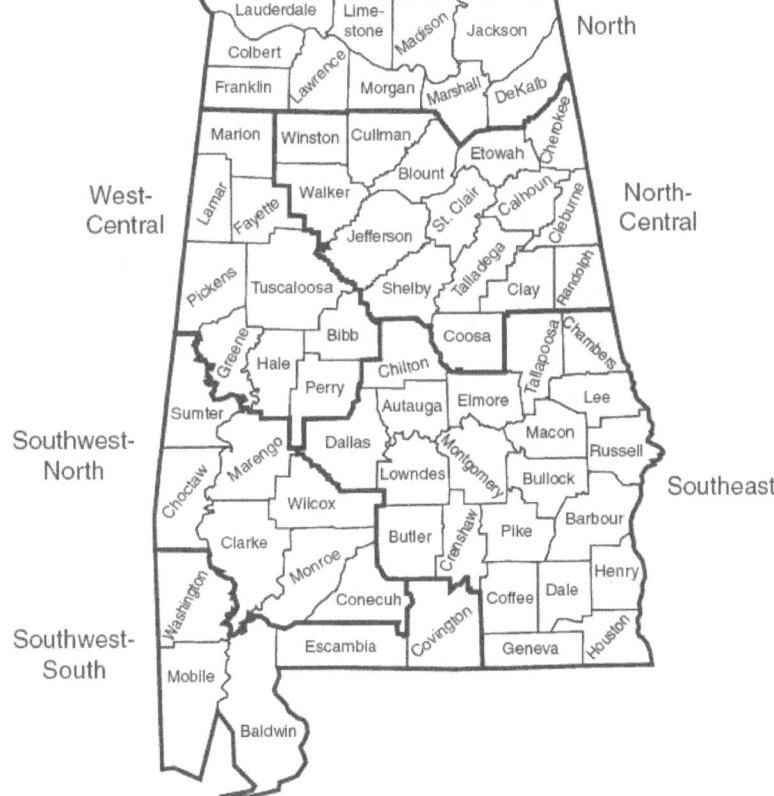

Figure 1—Forest survey regions in Alabama.

Growing stock denoted trees that were classified as having size, form, dimension, and soundness to produce commercial wood products. Timberlands were lands that were suitable for logging and capable of producing a sustainable crop of trees and not classified as reserve.

Both growing stock and timberland definitions changed over time, as harvesting and processing techniques evolved. For example, trees originally had to be 50 percent sound in order to be categorized as growing stock. In the 1980s this changed to 33 percent sound. Formulas and methodology for computing individual tree

volumes changed throughout the life of the survey as well. Many of these changes were precipitated by the advent of and constant improvement in computer technology.

Methodology used in collecting and processing inventory data has also changed. Various sampling schemes have been used over the last 70 years. Strips, fixed plots, and variable-radius plots have been installed across the State at one time or another. Variable-radius plots were utilized from 1972 to 1990, while the last two surveys have used a four-subplot fixed-radius design. Systems for determining forest area have evolved from interpretation of aerial photographs by FIA personnel to automated classification of satellite imagery. These changes help facilitate the collection and processing of data for the purpose of obtaining accurate assessment of the State's forests. However, the changes can confound long-term trend analysis, particularly for the average annual change variables—growth, removals, and mortality.

When possible, older data were reprocessed to account for some of these changes. This reprocessing failed to capture all changes and is not possible for data collected prior to 1972, as electronic datasets are not available for these surveys. Therefore, some caution is advised when comparing inventory data from different periods. Still, this information represents the best data available for describing the history of Alabama's forests.

Longleaf pine saplings in Baldwin County, 1897. (photo by Gifford Pinchot—founder of the USDA Forest Service, USDA Forest Service, Bugwood.org)

Total area of forest land in Alabama has steadily increased since 1936. In fact, the State's timberland base has grown 20 percent since that initial survey. The majority of the additional acreage was added between 1936 and 1963. Since 1963, total timberland area has never fluctuated by > 1.5 million acres. The 2005 estimate of 22.7 million acres is the second highest statewide estimate of forest land ever recorded for Alabama (fig. 2).

While total forest land area has remained stable since 1963, the area of planted stands has increased substantially. Planted stands were first identified as a separate classification during the 1972 survey. At that time, they accounted for 1.7 million acres, or about 8 percent of Alabama's timberland base. In 2005, more than one-quarter of Alabama's timberland area was in plantations with these stands occupying 6.3 million acres of timberland statewide.

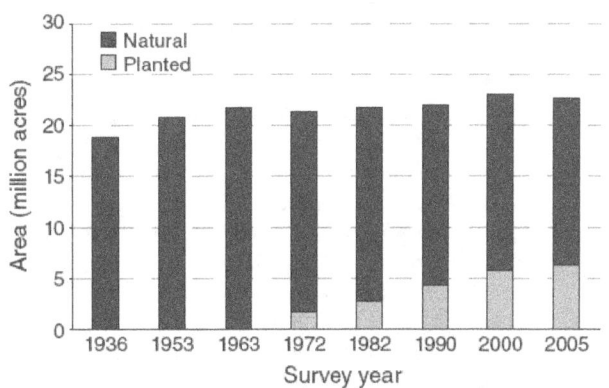

Figure 2—Area of forest land by survey year and stand origin, Alabama.

The increased prominence of pine plantations in Alabama has impacted forest-type distribution in the State. Many of the State's natural stands have been converted to plantations, particularly natural pine stands and oak-pine stands. Additionally, many lands that were under agriculture have been planted in pines and converted to forests. The area of natural loblolly pine

Nine-year-old longleaf pine stand after a snow in Randolph County. (photo by David Stephens, Bugwood.org)

stands has decreased over 46 percent since 1972, while the area of oak-pine stands has dropped 39 percent over the same period (fig. 3). Conversely, the area of planted loblolly pine forests has increased fivefold over the last 30 years. Oak-hickory forests have increased as well. There were 5.7 million acres of oak-hickory forests across the State in 1972. Today, there are 7.3 million, an increase of over 28 percent.

The loss in oak-gum-cypress forests and gain in elm-ash-cottonwood types are linked. Changes in FIA methodology and definitions often confound long-term analysis, and this is one such case. Earlier surveys typed almost all bottomland types as oak-gum-cypress. Current procedures type many of these stands as elm-ash-cottonwood. Therefore, it is often best to combine data for these two types when considering bottomland forest types. In 1972, these two types combined represented 2.5 million acres of Alabama's

forests. Today, they account for 2.7 million acres. Thus, there has been little overall change in area for Alabama's bottomland forests.

Most of Alabama's forest land loss occurred in the northern and northeastern portions of the State (fig. 4). There appears to be a correlation between the presence of large cities and interstate highways and loss of forest land. One area with significant deforestation is bracketed by I–65 to the west and I–20 to the east. Interstate 59 runs between the two. Two of the State's largest cities, Birmingham and Huntsville, lie in this area. The counties containing and surrounding the State's other two large cities, Montgomery and Mobile, also lost forest land. Both of these urban areas contain interstate highways as well. The combination of large cities and major roads appears to be a recipe for loss of forest land acreage (fig. 4).

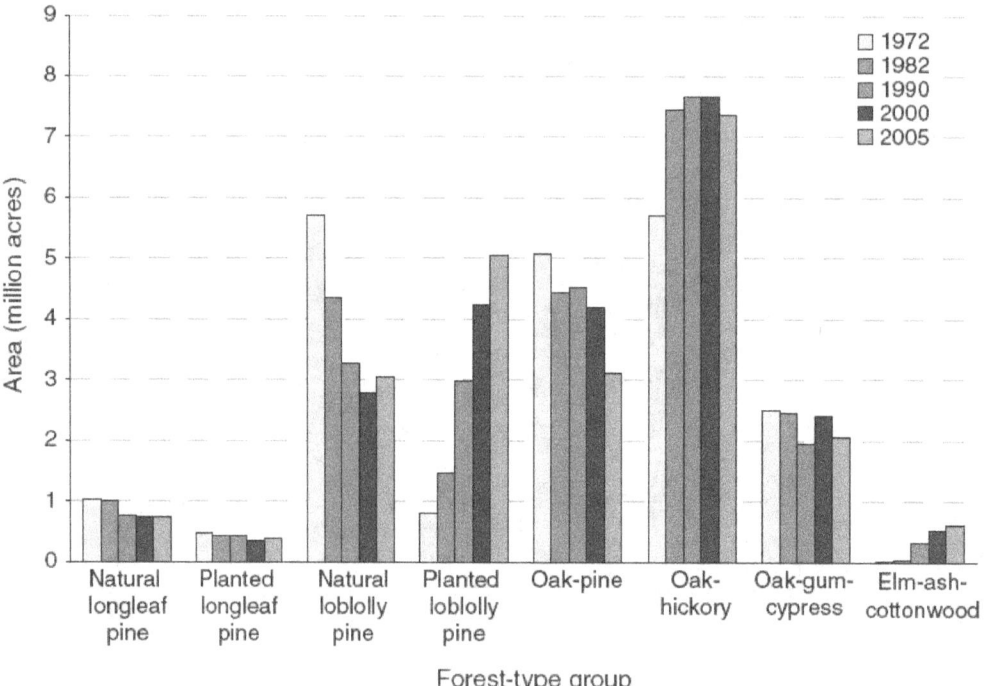

Figure 3—Area of forest land by forest-type group and survey year, Alabama.

Hardwood forest. (photo courtesy of the Alabama Forestry Commission)

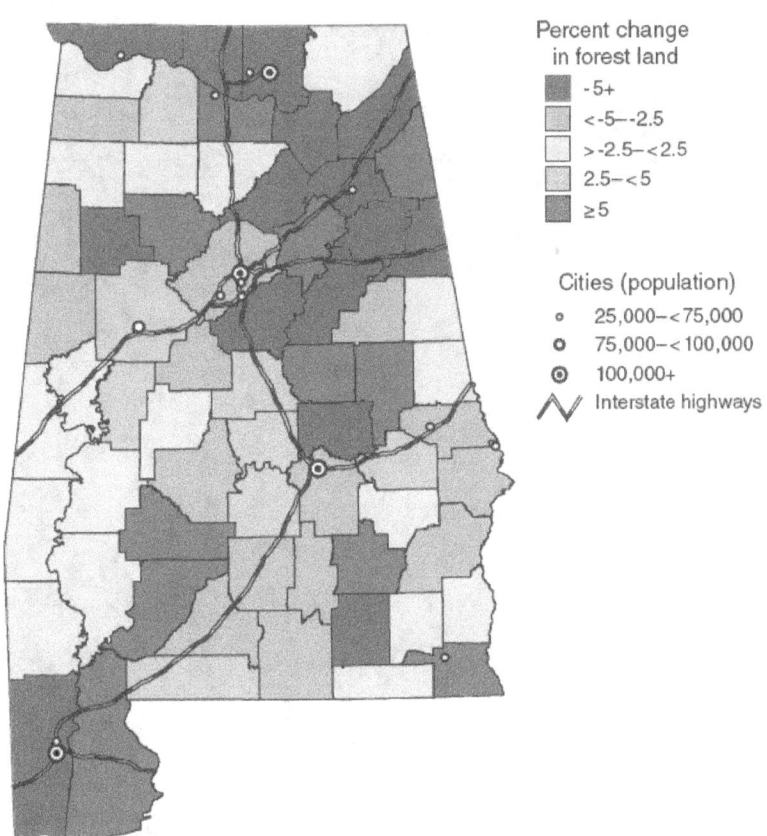

Percent change
in forest land

- -5+
- <-5--2.5
- >-2.5-<2.5
- 2.5-<5
- ≥5

Cities (population)

- 25,000-<75,000
- 75,000-<100,000
- 100,000+
- Interstate highways

Figure 4—Percent change in forest land area by
county, Alabama, 2000 to 2005.

The National Woodland Owner Survey (NWOS) (Butler and others 2005) conducted by the Forest Service is a nationwide effort to identify landowner opinions, goals, management styles, and concerns involving forest land in private ownership. Private landowners are important in Alabama because they own 95 percent of the State's forest area. The NWOS employed mail-out questionnaires and telephone surveys to obtain information about a sample of forest landowners. The objective was to better understand what is important to the owners of family forests, i.e., private individual forest ownerships, in the United States.

The NWOS sampled family forest owners in Alabama between 2002 and 2004. Summarized responses were developed from 197 returned questionnaires and 65 completed telephone surveys. Family forests were found to account for 15.3 million acres or 67 percent of the State's forest land. Businesses were found to own 28 percent and various Federal, State, and local government agencies the remaining 5 percent (table 1).

NWOS findings indicate that 432,000 family forest owners owned the 15.3 million acres of family forest in the State. Only 148,000 family forest owners owned at least 10 acres each, but these owners controlled 93 percent of the family forest land in Alabama. Only 53,000 family forest owners owned at least 50 acres each, but such tracts accounted for 78 percent of the State's family-owned forest acreage (table 2).

Catfish pond in Marshall County. (photo by Kelvin J. Daniels)

Table 1—Forest land area by ownership type, Alabama, 2004

| All ownerships | Public | | | | Private | | |
	Total[a]	Federal[a]	State[a]	Local[a]	Total[a]	Family	Business[b]
				thousand acres			
22,987	1,291	928	241	122	21,696	15,343	6,353

Numbers in rows may not sum to totals due to rounding.

[a] Forest resources of the United States, 2002 (Smith and others 2004).

[b] Includes corporations, nonfamily partnerships, tribal lands, nongovernmental organizations, clubs, and other nonfamily groups.

Table 2—Area and number of family-owned forests by size of forest landholdings, Alabama, 2004

| Size of forest landholdings | Area | | | Ownerships | | | Sample size |
acres	Acres	Standard error	Percent	Number	Standard error	Percent	number
	- - - - thousand - - - -			- - - - thousand - - - -			
1–9	996	315	6.5	284	84	65.9	17
10–49	2,342	402	15.3	95	16	22.1	40
50–99	1,347	342	8.8	21	4	4.9	23
100–499	4,802	489	31.3	26	3	6.1	82
500–999	1,815	373	11.8	3	<1	0.6	31
1,000–4,999	2,869	426	18.7	2	<1	0.4	49
5,000+	1,171	329	7.6	<1	<1	<0.1	20
Total	15,343	212	100.0	432	84	100.0	262

Acreage held for production of nontimber forest products was first, followed by acreage held for esthetics and acreage held for land investment. Acreage held for firewood and acreage held for timber production were smallest (table 3). However, stated reasons for owning forests may not be consistent with reported forest activities of family forest landowners. Timber harvest and tree planting ranked second and third in acres impacted, behind only private recreation. This indicates that the economic impacts of harvesting timber plays a larger role in landowner decisions than they originally assume (table 4).

Sweetgum and yellow-poplar are two of the more abundant hardwood species in Alabama. (photo courtesy of the Alabama Forestry Commission)

Table 3—Area and number of family-owned forests by reason for owning forest land, Alabama, 2004

Reason[a]	Area			Ownerships			Sample size
	Acres	Standard error	Percent	Number	Standard error	Percent	
	- - - - thousand - - - -			- - - - thousand - - - -			number
Esthetics	9,311	510	60.7	242	48	56.0	159
Nature protection	7,554	520	49.2	247	52	57.2	129
Land investment	9,194	511	59.9	188	45	43.5	157
Part of farm, home, or cabin[b]	4,216	474	27.5	192	49	44.4	72
Privacy	5,341	620	34.8	145	44	33.6	55
Family legacy	7,379	520	48.1	244	49	56.5	126
Nontimber forest products	10,599	487	69.1	230	47	53.2	181
Firewood production	1,347	342	8.8	13	4	3.0	23
Timber production	1,405	346	9.2	14	4	3.2	24
Hunting or fishing	8,257	519	53.8	53	11	12.3	141
Other recreation	7,671	520	50.0	74	17	17.1	131
No answer	4,568	483	29.8	87	26	20.1	78

Numbers include landowners who ranked each objective as very important (1) or important (2) on a seven-point Likert scale.
[a] Categories are not exclusive.
[b] Includes primary and secondary residences.

Table 4—Area and number of family-owned forests by recent (past 5 years) forestry activity, Alabama, 2004

Activity[a]	Area			Ownerships			Sample size
	Acres	Standard error	Percent	Number	Standard error	Percent	
	- - - thousand - - -			- - - - thousand - - - -			number
Timber harvest	8,453	562	55.1	98	37	22.7	119
Collection of NTFP	923	327	6.0	9	3	2.1	13
Site preparation	5,095	495	33.2	11	3	2.5	87
Tree planting	6,969	518	45.4	52	16	12.0	119
Fire hazard reduction	4,919	491	32.1	48	23	11.1	84
Application of chemicals	4,451	480	29.0	34	14	7.9	76
Road/trail maintenance	6,266	513	40.8	32	12	7.4	107
Wildlife habitat improvement	4,978	492	32.4	23	5	5.3	85
Posting land	5,535	625	36.1	49	23	11.3	57
Private recreation	8,740	642	57.0	120	38	27.8	90
Public recreation	1,068	377	7.0	1	1	0.2	11
Cost share	2,460	408	16.0	36	29	8.3	42
Conservation easement[b]	410	153	2.7	10	10	2.3	7
Green certification[b]	1,054	320	6.9	1	1	0.2	18

NTFP = nontimber forest products.
[a] Categories are not exclusive.
[b] Not limited to past 5 years.

The State's total growing-stock volume has increased dramatically since the 1953 survey. Part of this increase may be attributed to changes in the methods used to compute tree volumes that occurred between the 1990 and 2000 surveys. Preliminary analyses indicate that would account for only a 5- to 8-percent increase. However, the same procedures and formulas were used in both 2000 and 2005. Therefore, changes that occurred between the last two surveys, and any large changes between the current inventory and older surveys, are indicative of real changes in Alabama's forest structure (fig. 5).

Softwood volume increased 140 percent since 1953, while hardwood volume rose 143 percent. The largest jump in softwood

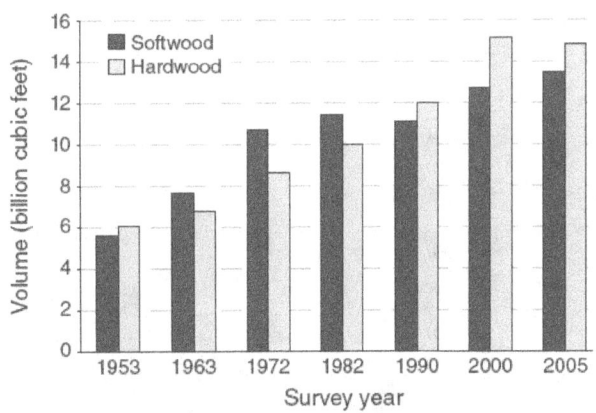

Figure 5—Volume of growing stock on timberland by survey year and species group, Alabama.

Loblolly pine, as found in this 26-year-old stand in Randolph County, is the predominant softwood species in Alabama. (photo by David Stephens, Bugwood.org)

volume occurred between 1953 and 1972, as 65 percent of the volume increase between 1953 and 2005 occurred prior to 1982. Softwood volume increased 6 percent over the last 5 years.

Hardwood volume increased 11 percent between the 1953 and 1963 surveys. Starting with the 1972 inventory, hardwood volume across the State began to increase dramatically. Hardwood growing-stock volume rose 75 percent between the 1972

Waterfall in Colbert County. (photo by Kelvin J. Daniels)

and 2000 inventories. The 2005 survey was the first to show a decrease in hardwood growing-stock volume. Hardwood growing-stock volume was estimated at 14.8 billion cubic feet, down 2 percent since the 2000 inventory.

All-live softwood volume in the lower diameter classes has jumped considerably the past two surveys. Between the 2000 and 2005 inventories, volume in the 8- and 10-inch diameter classes rose 11 percent and 13 percent, respectively. The 2005 estimate of all-live volume for softwoods in the 8-inch class is 43 percent higher than the 1990 estimate, while the 10-inch class has had a 33-percent increase over the same period. This increase in volume for softwood species < 14 inches in diameter can be attributed directly to the establishment of pine plantations (fig. 6).

Compared to the estimate of volume from the 2000 inventory, the volume in the middle-to-upper diameter classes, 14 to 28 inches, has remained fairly constant. However, the data indicate that, over the long term, there is now more volume in these diameter classes than ever before. For example, the 2005 volume of 20-inch trees is 82 percent higher than the 1972 estimate.

All-live hardwood volume of Alabama's forests has risen as well. However, unlike softwood volume, which has a spike in the lower diameter classes, hardwood volume has been increasing over all diameter classes for the last 30 years. This increase is proportional to tree size. For example, hardwood volume in the 12-inch class is

53 percent higher than in 1972. The 2005 inventory volumes in the 16-, 20-, and 24-inch classes were 91 percent, 167 percent, and 241 percent greater, respectively, than the corresponding 1972 estimates (fig. 7).

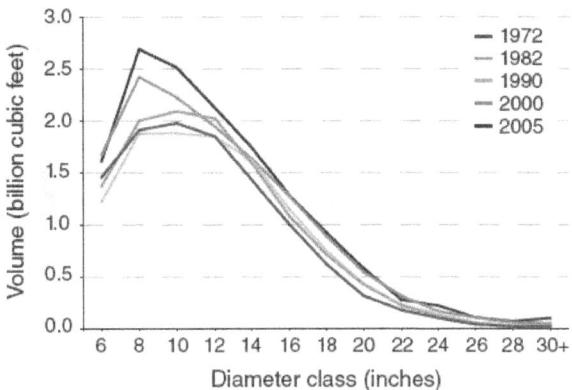

Figure 6—Volume of all-live softwoods on forest land by diameter class and survey year, Alabama.

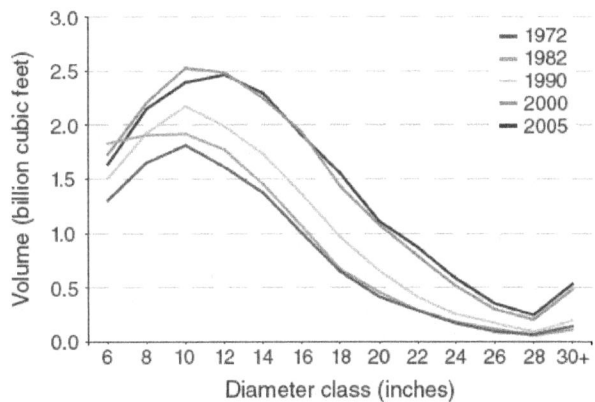

Figure 7—Volume of all-live hardwoods on forest land by diameter class and survey year, Alabama.

The 2005 inventory estimate of hardwood volume largely mirrors the 2000 inventory numbers. The 2005 inventory estimates of volume in the 8- and 10-inch diameter classes are 2.5 to 5 percent lower than the corresponding estimates from the 2000 inventory. The two lines converge at the 12-inch class and follow each other from that point on. The 2005 inventory volume estimates are slightly higher for all diameter classes > 18 inches.

At the time of the 2005 inventory, all-live softwood volume was distributed unevenly across the State. It was greatest in the southwest portion of the State and lowest in the northern counties. The counties with the most softwood volume were Baldwin, Choctaw, Clarke, Monroe, and Washington (fig. 8).

At the time of the 2005 inventory, hardwoods occurred across the State. All-live hardwood volume by county increased slightly from east to west, but the trend may be largely an artifact of county size. It should be noted that hardwood volume was highest in the northern counties where softwood volume was lowest, and in the southwestern corner of the State where softwood volume was highest. Indeed, three of the five counties that had the highest all-live hardwood volume also had the highest softwood volume. These counties were Baldwin, Clarke, and Monroe. Tuscaloosa and Jackson were the other two counties that had the highest all-live hardwood volume (fig. 9).

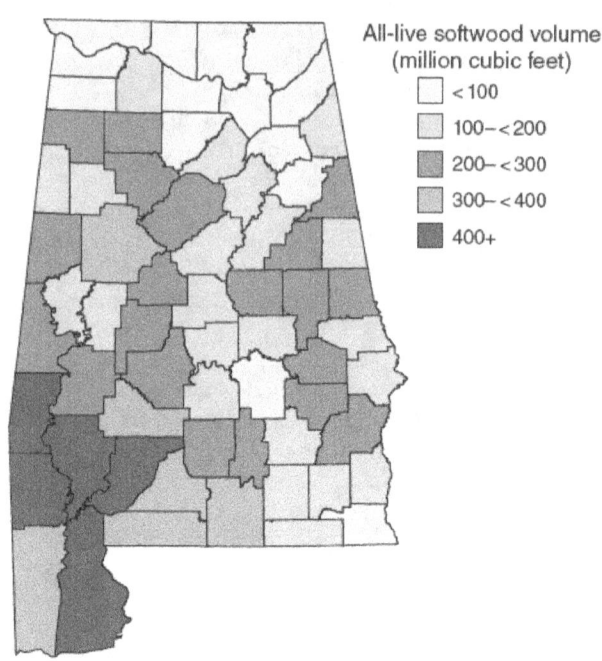

Figure 8—Total all-live volume of softwoods on forest land by county, Alabama, 2005.

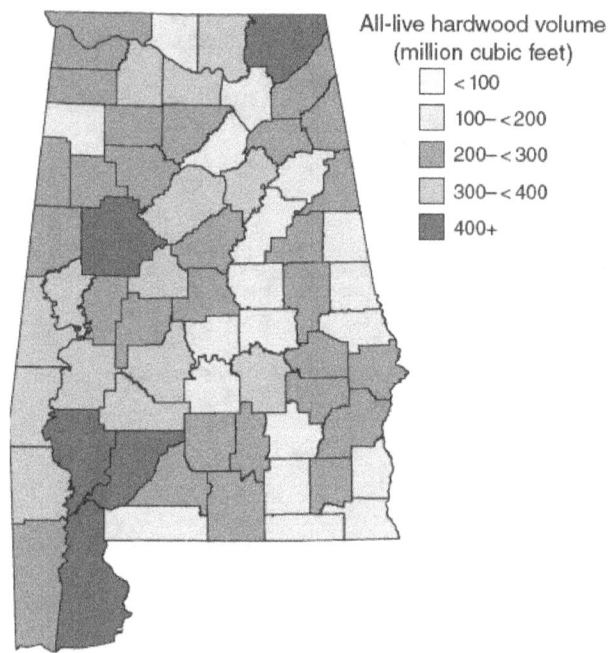

Figure 9—Total all-live volume of hardwoods on forest land by county, Alabama, 2005.

Loblolly pine is the predominant softwood species in Alabama, accounting for 10.2 billion cubic feet, or 72 percent, of all-live softwood volume. The current inventory of loblolly pine is 2.5 times as great as that of all other softwoods combined. Loblolly pine is the only softwood species that has increased in volume substantially over the last 5 years. Volumes of all other softwood species either declined or remained constant. In fact, the recent increase in the volume of loblolly pine, 1.2 billion cubic feet, was more than the current standing volume of any other softwood species (fig. 10).

Loblolly pine stand on the Westervelt Management Area in Pickens County. (photo by Kelvin J. Daniels)

13

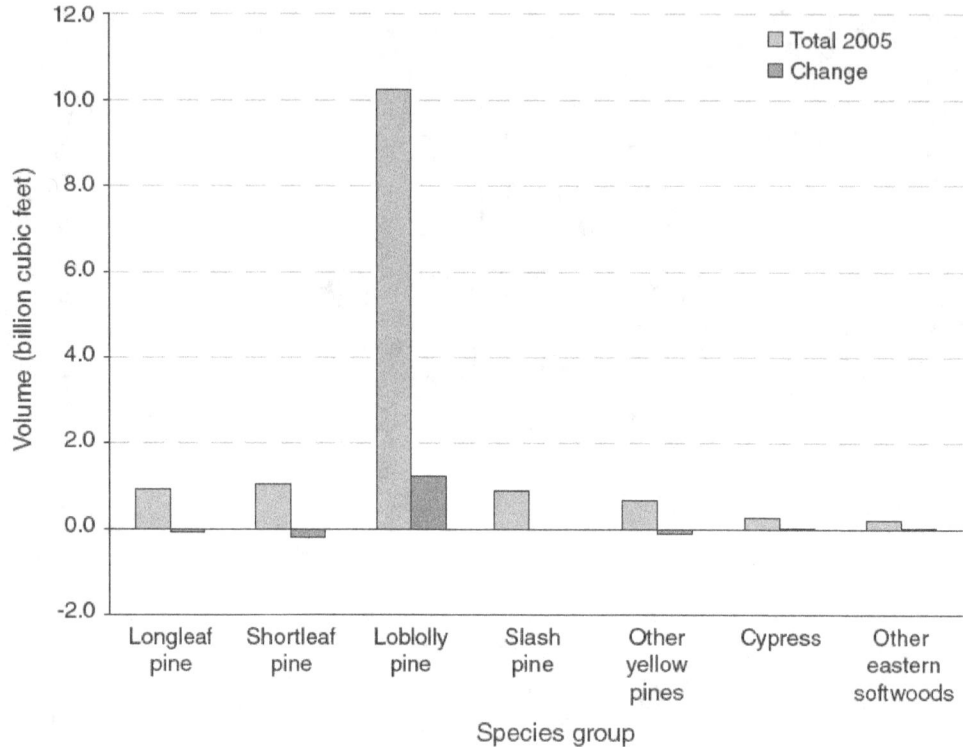

Figure 10—Volume of all-live softwood on forest land by species group, Alabama, 2005, and change since 2000.

The species with the greatest loss in volume is shortleaf pine. The current estimate of 1.1 billion cubic feet is 192 million cubic feet less than the 2000 estimate. Longleaf pine ranked second in softwood volume loss. The volume of longleaf pine fell from 1.0 billion cubic feet to 926 million cubic feet in just 5 years, a decline of nearly 8 percent.

Unlike its softwood resource, Alabama's hardwood resource is not dominated by a single species. The other red oak group contains the most all-live volume, 4.1 billion cubic feet, followed by sweetgum with 2.7 billion cubic feet. Hickory, select white oak, and yellow-poplar form a third tier, with the volume of these species ranging from 1.5 billion to 1.6 billion cubic feet (fig. 11).

Select red oak, tupelo-blackgum, and select white oak groups declined in all-live volume since 2000. Select red oak and tupelo-blackgum lost 55 million cubic feet each, while select white oak lost 41 million cubic feet. The select red oak group was impacted most, as the decrease in volume represented more than an 8-percent loss since the 2000 estimate.

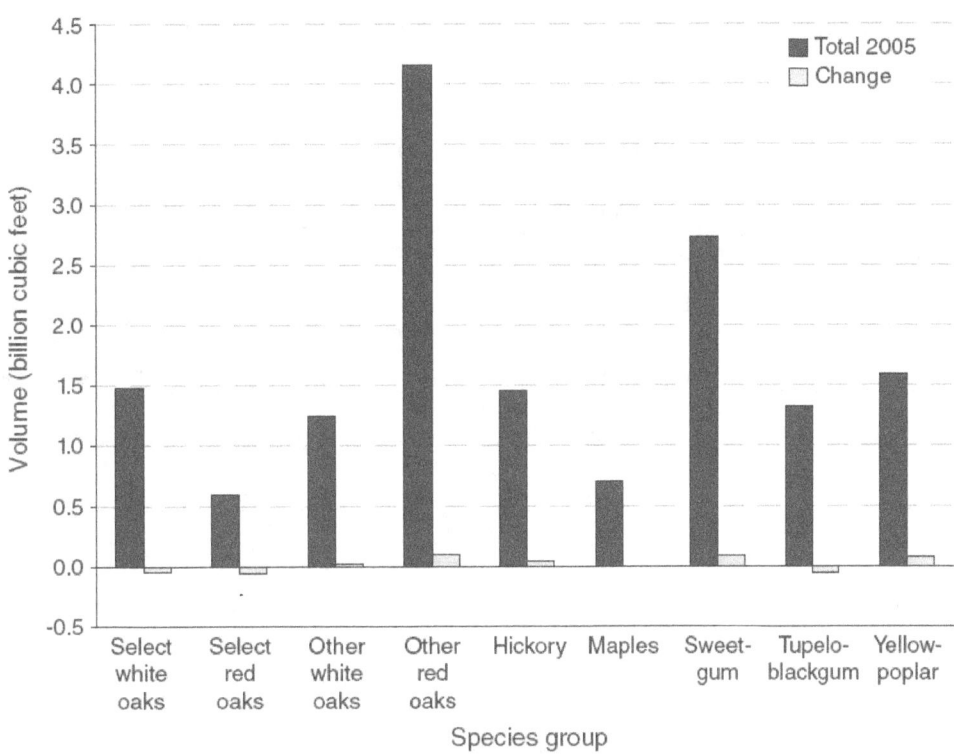

Figure 11—Volume of all-live hardwood on forest land by species group, Alabama, 2005, and change since 2000.

Oak-hickory stands account for more area of Alabama's forests than any other type. (photo by Andrew J. Hartsell)

Prescribed fire in a sapling longleaf pine stand on Escambia Experimental Forest in Alabama. (photo by William D. Boyer, USDA Forest Service, Bugwood.org)

Currently, 995.2 million cubic feet of softwood volume is produced each year in Alabama, a 13-percent increase in annual volume increment over the prior inventory period. Conversely, 827.4 million cubic feet are removed each year in timber harvest operations, a 7-percent decline from the earlier survey. The 2005 survey marks the first time that average annual growing-stock growth-to-removals ratio for softwoods has exceeded one in over 30 years. This is the result of both an increase in growth and the first ever decrease in removals of softwood in the State (fig. 12).

The State's current softwood growth-to-removals ratio is 1.2. This means that for every cubic foot of softwood volume removed from Alabama's forests, 1.2 cubic feet are grown. From 1972 until the present inventory, the growth-to-removals ratio for these species had ranged from 0.9 to 1.0.

Alabama is growing 58 percent more softwood volume each year than it grew during the 1953 to 1962 period. Softwood harvest has risen over 168 percent over the same timeframe. Most of this production is due to the establishment of pine plantations.

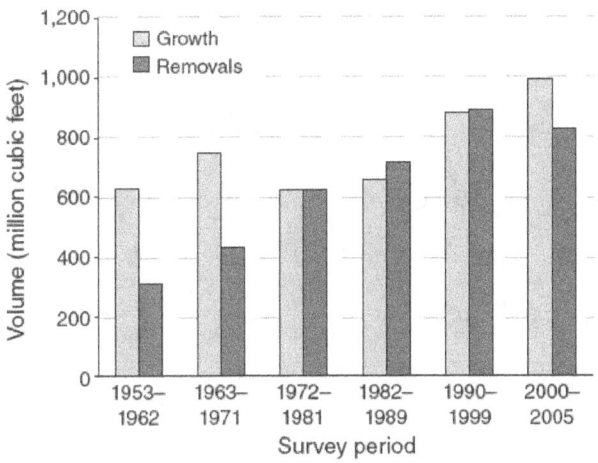

Figure 12—Average annual growth and average annual removals of softwood growing stock on timberland, by survey period, Alabama.

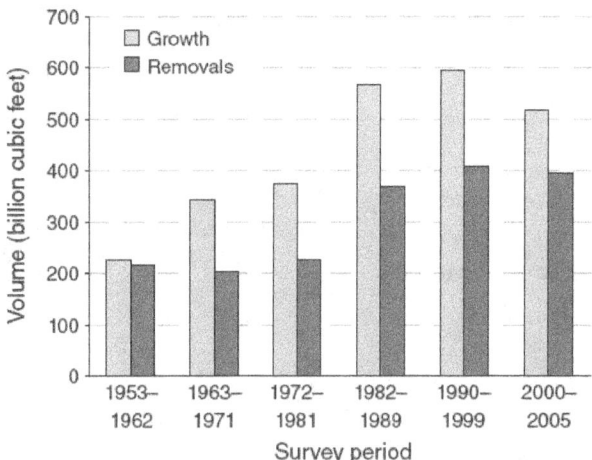

Figure 13—Average annual growth and average annual removals of hardwood growing stock on timberland, by survey period, Alabama.

Alabama's forests have historically produced more hardwood growing-stock volume than has been removed. The latest survey results are no different. Presently, 517 million cubic feet of hardwood is grown each year in Alabama, while 394 million cubic feet is removed. Until the current survey, each inventory period reported increases in hardwood growth. Hardwood removals increased with each succeeding survey with the exception of the survey period 1963–1971 and the 2005 survey. The current results show a decrease in both of these metrics. Hardwood growing-stock growth decreased 13 percent since the 1990 to 1999 survey, while total removals are down by 3 percent (fig. 13).

The current growth-to-removals ratio for the State's hardwoods is 1.3, indicating that for every cubic foot of hardwood cut, 1.3 cubic feet is grown. This is the lowest ratio in almost half a century. This ratio has steadily decreased with each successive inventory. The 1963 to 1971 ratio was 1.6, and the ratio has dropped steadily since that time.

Growth of Alabama's softwoods was not distributed evenly across all tree sizes. Seventy-five percent of all-live softwood growth occurred in the first three diameter classes, declining sharply beyond the 10-inch class. Indeed, softwood growth in the 14-inch diameter class is less than one-third of the growth in the 10-inch category. Much of this growth can be attributed to the vigor of the younger, smaller diameter trees that are typical of pine plantations. Less than 8 percent of softwood growth occurred in trees in the ≥ 16-inch diameter class, and < 2 percent occurred in trees > 19 inches (fig. 14).

All-live removals exhibit a similar pattern, offset by one diameter class. Over one-half of the softwood removals are found in the 8- through 12-inch class trees. This jumps to over 65 percent when the smallest diameter class is included. Only 23 percent of total softwood removals occurred in the ≥ 16-inch class trees.

Live softwood growth exceeded removals for just the first three size classes. Starting with the 12-inch class, removals exceeded growth. Pine plantations contribute to this scenario. These intensively managed stands emphasize younger, faster growing trees, i.e., those that are ≤ 12 inches diameter at breast height (d.b.h.). Shorter rotations, 18 to 25 years, produce stands of pines ranging from 10 to 16 inches d.b.h. The cycle is then reset as these stands are harvested and replanted.

Growth of live hardwoods in Alabama is skewed to the smaller diameter classes as well, but not nearly as much as growth of softwoods. Thirty-eight percent of the hardwood growth occurs in the first two diameter classes, and over one-half occurs in the first three classes, compared to softwood growth, which has 55 and 75 percent, respectively, in these categories. This growth in smaller diameter trees can be attributed to the growth vigor of younger trees. Alabama's hardwoods, unlike the State's softwoods, exhibited substantial growth in the upper diameter classes. Twenty-four percent of all hardwood growth occurs in trees that are in the ≥ 16-inch class, compared to only 8 percent for softwoods. In hardwoods, 11 percent of growth occurs in trees in the ≥20-inch class, while <2 percent of softwood growth occurs in trees in this size range (fig. 15).

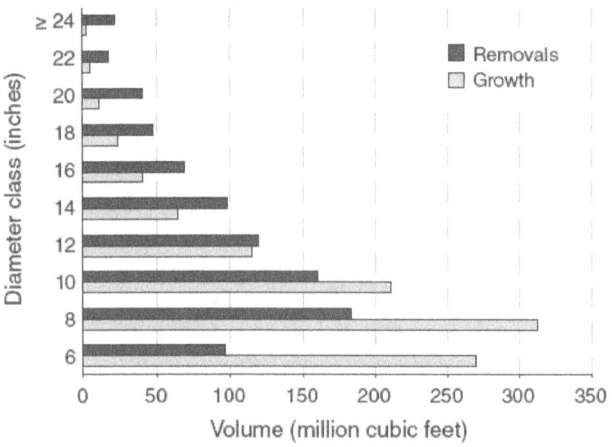

Figure 14—Average annual growth and average annual removals of live softwoods by diameter class on forest land, Alabama, 2000 to 2005.

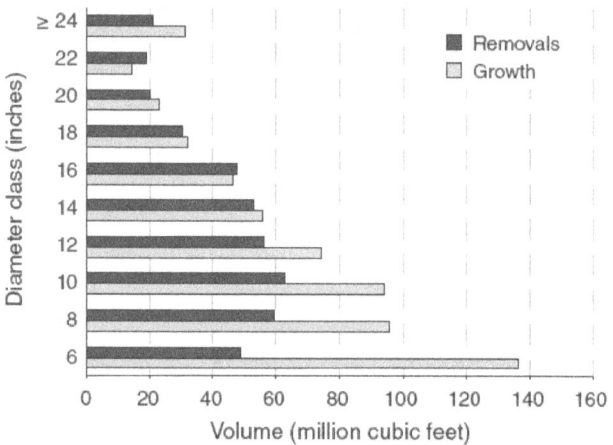

Figure 15—Average annual growth and average annual removals of live hardwoods by diameter class on forest land, Alabama, 2000 to 2005.

A well stocked softwood plantation in Escambia County, Alabama, T.R. Miller company, November 1963. (photo by William D. Boyer, USDA Forest Service, Bugwood.org)

In Alabama, hardwood removals volume is distributed across tree sizes more widely than is softwood removals volume. Although hardwood removals volume is concentrated in the smaller diameter classes, a significant portion of it occurs in diameter classes > 10 inches. Forty-one percent of hardwood removals occur in the 6-, 8-, and 10-inch classes. However, 33 percent of removals occur in trees ≥ 16-inch class.

Average annual growth of live hardwoods exceeds average annual removals for all diameter classes except the 16- and 22-inch classes. The greatest divergence between growth and removals appears in the smaller classes. For example, growth in the 6-inch class is almost three times as great as removals in that class.

There are only two counties in Alabama—Morgan and Winston—in which removals exceed growth for live softwoods. Interestingly, except for Baldwin County, the counties with the highest growth-to-removals ratios are not those where the most volume is present. Most of the highest ranked counties occur in the eastern portion of the State, and a few are in the northern section where softwood volumes were low (fig. 16).

Hardwood growth-to-removals ratios are > 0 for all Alabama counties, indicating that hardwoods are growing faster than they are harvested. There appears to be no correlation between location and growth-to-removals ratios for all-live hardwoods, due to the common occurrence of these species across the State (fig. 17).

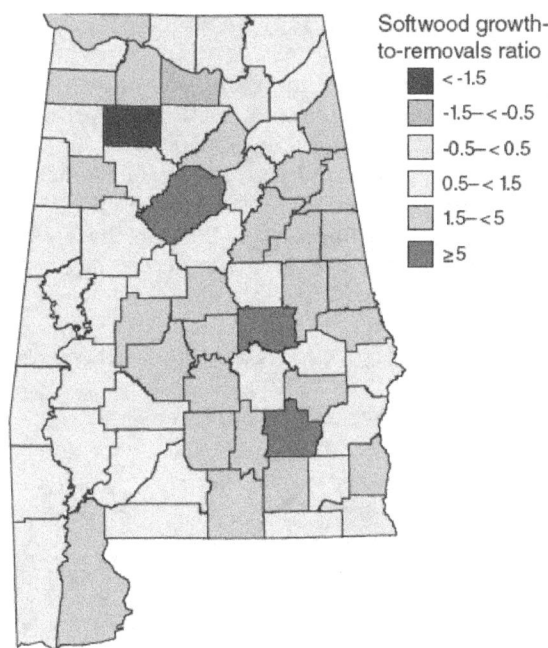

Figure 16—All-live softwood growth-to-removals ratio on forest land, Alabama, 2005.

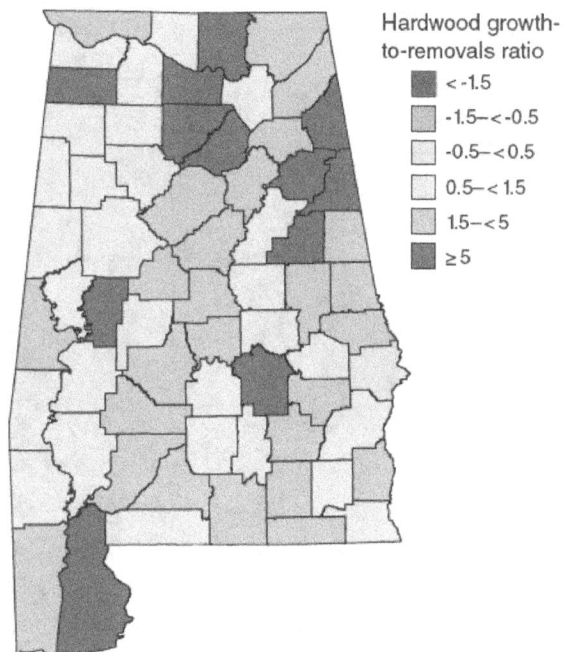

Figure 17—All-live hardwood growth-to-removals ratio on forest land, Alabama, 2005.

Stands classified as plantations currently account for over one-fourth of Alabama's forest area. The long-term consequences of southern pine plantation forestry are a topic of debate among environmentalists, industrialists, academics, and professional land managers. FIA data can be used to quantify the impacts and benefits that this type of forest management has on the State's natural resources.

How productive are Alabama's southern pine plantations? While plantations occupy only 28 percent of the forest area of the

State, they contain 40 percent of the State's all-live softwood volume. Moreover, plantations account for 67 percent of the annual growth and 55 percent of the annual removals of softwood species. Thus, plantations increase the efficiency of timber production statewide (table 5).

Species diversity is lower in planted stands than in natural pine stands, so replacement of natural pine stands by planted stands is a subject of environmental concern. Loblolly pine is the predominant species in planted stands, accounting for 84 percent of the all-live volume in plantations. Ninety-two percent of the softwood volume in plantations can be attributed to this one species.

Conversely, 67 percent of the all-live volume in natural stands is from hardwood species. Natural stands account for 97 percent of the State's hardwood volume and 93 percent of the average annual growth. Other red oaks represent the largest species group in this category, representing 23 percent of the total hardwood volume in natural stands. Sweetgum is second at 15 percent.

These stands are not dominated by deciduous trees alone. Sixty percent of the State's softwood volume is found in natural stands. Almost all of the shortleaf and longleaf pine stands occur in these forests, as well as hemlock, cypress, and other softwood species.

Plantations may be more efficient at growing pines, particularly loblolly, but are they more vulnerable to disease and pests? In fact, plantation management is very effective in reducing tree mortality. Mortality-to-volume ratios for both management regimes are low, but the mortality-to-volume ratio for loblolly pine in plantations is 0.006, compared to 0.02 in natural stands.

Over one-fourth of the State's forests are comprised of pine plantations, such as this one in Marshall County. (photo by Kelvin J. Daniels)

Table 5—Standing volume, average annual growth, average annual removals, and average annual mortality of all-live trees on forest land by species group and stand origin, Alabama, 2005

Species group	Natural				Planted			
	Volume	Growth	Removals	Mortality	Volume	Growth	Removals	Mortality
				million cubic feet				
Softwood								
Shortleaf pine	1,019.6	22.9	42.3	25.4	40.8	4.7	22.6	0.8
Slash pine	564.8	27.3	28.9	4.3	311.6	31.1	27.9	2.0
Longleaf pine	888.3	21.4	21.6	13.2	37.8	3.4	17.7	0.1
Loblolly pine	4,983.9	261.0	285.4	104.2	5,243.7	662.1	375.8	31.2
Other yellow pines	635.8	0.0	18.8	35.4	28.9	5.0	8.1	0.1
Eastern hemlock	28.5	0.0	0.1	0.3	—	—	—	—
Cypress	267.4	6.1	0.5	1.3	3.5	0.1	0.2	0.0
Other eastern softwoods	192.7	9.1	2.4	1.0	6.4	0.5	0.5	0.1
Total softwoods	8,580.9	347.8	400.0	185.2	5,672.7	706.9	452.9	34.2
Hardwood								
Select white oaks	1,452.0	43.0	28.7	11.5	31.0	2.3	7.9	0.2
Select red oaks	587.3	11.6	3.9	6.4	12.5	-2.7	3.3	4.2
Other white oaks	1,234.1	42.9	13.4	5.3	17.5	1.1	5.9	0.3
Other red oaks	4,011.2	128.5	97.6	64.8	143.4	11.4	27.7	1.3
Hickory	1,427.8	36.4	21.7	11.5	32.3	2.9	6.1	0.3
Hard maple	92.5	2.4	1.0	1.1	0.1	-0.1	0.1	0.1
Soft maple	587.8	22.2	11.8	8.3	20.4	1.8	3.5	0.3
Beech	211.4	4.2	2.4	1.6	5.7	0.3	2.3	0.0
Sweetgum	2,603.3	91.9	59.2	23.6	124.8	12.6	16.8	0.6
Tupelo and blackgum	1,323.0	31.8	13.8	6.6	7.0	0.6	4.1	0.1
Ash	424.9	12.4	4.6	2.9	7.4	0.4	0.5	0.0
Cottonwood and aspen	36.0	2.8	0.5	0.2	0.1	0.0	0.2	0.1
Basswood	65.7	0.9	0.2	0.2	0.0	0.0	0.0	0.0
Yellow-poplar	1,519.1	67.7	25.5	9.6	72.1	6.1	9.2	1.5
Black walnut	22.3	0.9	0.0	0.1	0.2	0.1	0.0	0.0
Other eastern soft hardwoods	1,460.0	53.6	28.0	19.4	47.4	3.7	7.7	0.4
Other eastern hard hardwoods	177.9	1.6	3.0	5.2	6.4	0.4	1.4	0.2
Eastern noncommercial hardwoods	329.4	7.0	4.7	9.2	9.1	0.1	1.6	0.8
Total hardwoods	17,565.7	561.8	319.9	187.5	537.4	41.1	98.4	10.3
Total	26,146.6	909.6	719.9	372.7	6,210.0	747.9	551.3	44.6

— = no sample for the cell; 0.0 = a value of > 0.0 but < 0.05 for the cell.

Another topic of heated discussion is the contrast between diameter distributions in natural stands and in plantations. In planted stands, all-live softwood volume peaks in the 8-inch class, at over 1.8 billion cubic feet, and declines sharply thereafter. Seventy-five percent of the all-live softwood volume in planted stands is in the 6-, 8-, and 10-inch diameter classes. Only 11.5 percent of the total softwood volume in plantations is in the ≥ 14-inch diameter classes. No softwood trees in classes greater than the 26-inch class were recorded in planted stands during the 2005 survey period (fig. 18).

All-live softwood volume in natural stands is more broadly distributed across diameter classes and peaks in the 12- and 14-inch diameter classes. The volume in each of these two classes is around 1.4 billion cubic feet. Fifty-four percent of the live softwood

volume in natural stands occurs in the ≥ 14-inch classes. This is quite a contrast with the 11.5 percent for planted stands.

As described earlier, almost all of Alabama's hardwood trees are found in natural stands. Therefore, comparing hardwood volume in plantations with that in natural stands is unnecessary. Volume peaks around the 12-inch class. Fifty-three percent of hardwood volume occurs in ≥ 14-inch classes (fig. 19).

Plantations in Alabama are composed almost entirely of loblolly pine. These plantations contain and produce more volume than natural stands and have a lower mortality-to-volume ratio. Natural stands tend to have a greater variety of species, especially hardwoods, and have a greater proportion of their trees in larger diameter classes.

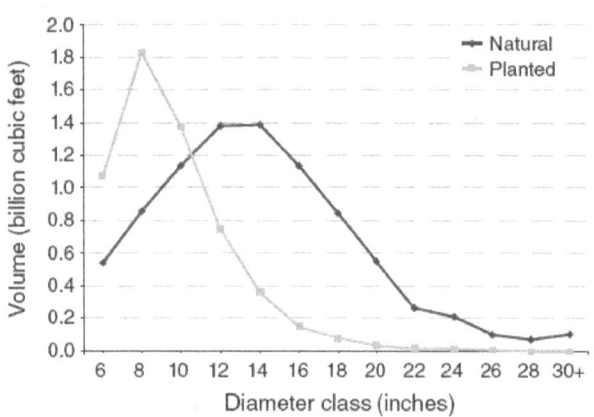

Figure 18—Volume of all-live softwoods on forest land, by diameter class and stand origin, Alabama, 2005.

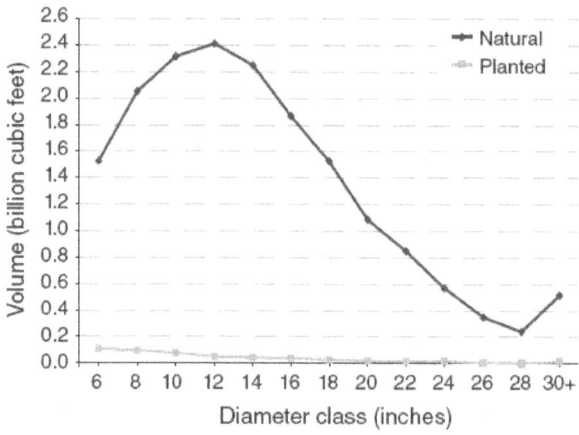

Figure 19—Volume of all-live hardwoods on forest land, by diameter class and stand origin, Alabama, 2005.

The health and condition of America's forests have always been of major concern to the Forest Service, as well as the scientific community and the public at large. The Forest Health Monitoring (FHM) Program was created to study the condition and long-term health of this country's forest lands. FHM was merged with FIA in 2000, as both programs shared many features. FHM information is collected on a subset of FIA plots. About 1 out of 16 FIA plots is selected for additional forest health sampling. Between 2001 and 2005, 239 forest health plots were installed with FIA plots across Alabama. Information from both sets of data, FIA and FHM, can be used to make inferences about the health of the State's forests.

Mortality

Average annual mortality, collected on all remeasured FIA plots, is the metric used to describe trees that die from natural causes such as insects, disease, fire, competition, weather, or old age. The average annual mortality of all-live hardwood and softwood trees in Alabama has generally increased with each successive survey, except for the 1990 survey. During the most recent survey period, annual mortality of softwood and annual mortality of hardwood trees averaged 219.4 cubic feet and 197.8 million cubic feet, respectively. Mean annual mortality of softwoods was up 31 percent since the previous survey, and hardwood mortality was up 18 percent. Since 1972, Alabama softwood and hardwood mortality have increased 304 and 88 percent, respectively (fig. 20).

Alabama Forestry Commission personnel working to control a fire. (photo courtesy of the Alabama Forestry Commission)

The 2001 to 2005 survey was the first time that softwood mortality exceeded mortality of hardwoods. Hardwood and softwood mortality rates had been about equal during the last inventory period.

The previous figure highlighted the fact that total average annual mortality of all-live species was rising in Alabama. But how much of this is due to the increase in live-tree volume and how big is the impact of these losses? The best way to answer

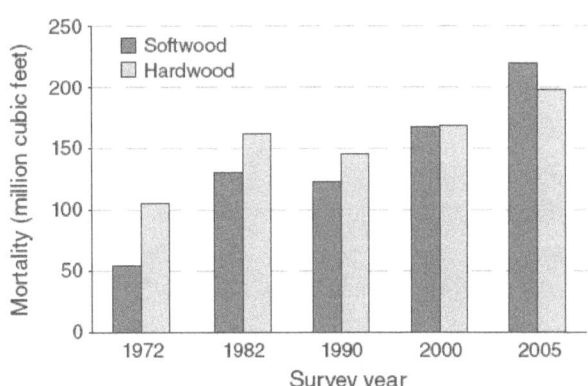

Figure 20—Average annual mortality of all-live trees on forest land, by survey year and species group, Alabama.

these questions is to compute the volume-to-mortality ratio for the State. This ratio describes the impact that average annual mortality has upon the current standing volume of trees, and to what degree this mortality impacts the forest resources of the State.

The current volume-to-mortality ratios for softwood and hardwoods in Alabama are 1:015 and 1:011, respectively. Thus, just over 1.5 percent of the standing volume of softwoods and 1 percent of the volume of hardwood dies each year (fig. 21).

Although the all-live volume of the State's forests has increased since 1972, the average annual mortality has increased at a greater

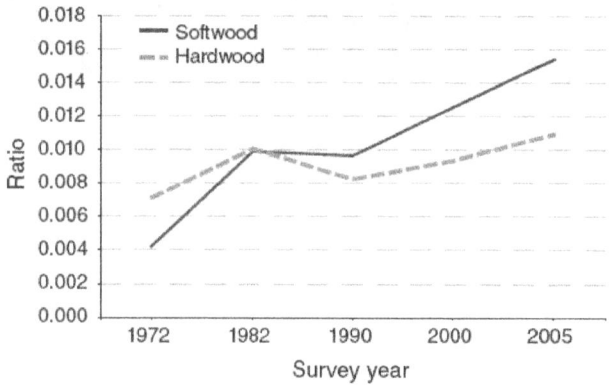

Figure 21—Average annual mortality-to-volume ratios of all-live trees on forest land, by survey year and species group, Alabama.

rate. The reasons for this are unknown. Older stands may have been understocked while current stands may be suffering from the effects of competition. Many factors may be influencing these results, including the impacts of human activity and development. The FHM plots recently established provide a baseline of data regarding the health of Alabama's forests. Future reports will provide trend analyses to help describe the state of health for Alabama's forests.

Average annual mortality of all-live trees on Alabama's forests has increased 25 percent over the last 5 years, from 334.7 million cubic feet per year to 417.2 million cubic feet per year. Insects are the primary reason for this rise in tree mortality, as average annual mortality due to insects rose nearly 200 percent, from 39 million cubic feet per year to over 115 million. Losses due to disease contributed an additional 106.2 million cubic feet over the last 5 years (table 6).

The primary causes of mortality differ for hardwood and softwood species. Interestingly, loss caused by insects is ranked lowest among hardwood species and highest for softwoods. Insects accounted for 114 million cubic feet of softwood loss each year. This is a dramatic increase since

Table 6—Average annual mortality of all-live trees on forest land by agent, survey period, and species group, Alabama

Agent	1990–1999			2000–2005		
	All species	Softwood	Hardwood	All species	Softwood	Hardwood
			million cubic feet			
Insect	38.7	38.0	0.7	115.1	114.4	0.7
Disease	95.5	36.3	59.2	106.3	28.6	77.8
Fire	4.8	2.1	2.6	4.2	1.2	3.0
Animal	5.7	0.5	5.2	10.8	1.7	9.1
Weather	113.6	52.8	60.8	75.7	29.0	46.7
Vegetation	32.4	21.0	11.4	44.0	18.3	25.7
Other/unknown	44.0	16.2	27.9	61.1	26.3	34.8
Total	334.7	166.9	167.8	417.2	219.4	197.8

the previous inventory and is the primary reason why softwood mortality exceeds hardwood. Insects account for over one-half of softwood mortality statewide. The southern pine beetle (*Dendroctonous frontalis* Zimmermann) and associated insects are responsible for the majority of insect-caused softwood mortality in the South. Disease and weather are the two main agents of death among Alabama's hardwoods. These two factors caused 63 percent of the hardwood mortality over the last 5 years.

Down Woody Material

Down woody material (DWM) is a measurement of the fallen trees, dead branches, leaves, and litter on the forest floor (Stolte 2001). DWM is a key component in many ecosystem functions such as nutrient cycling, carbon sequestering, wildlife and insect habitat, soil erosion, and fire behavior. Currently, FIA collects data on the extent and distribution of DWM across the Nation.

DWM is divided into five categories: (1) fine woody debris (FWD), (2) coarse woody debris (CWD), (3) litter, (4) duff, and (5) slash. FWD is comprised of small branches and trees < 3 inches in diameter. Tree sections and branches ≥ 3 inches in diameter are considered CWD. CWD is at least 3 feet in length. The litter layer of a forest floor is composed of freshly fallen leaves, cones, twigs, needles, pieces of bark, moss, lichens, and other such material. The duff is the organic layer that exists between the litter and mineral soil, and is derived from decomposing material from the litter layer. Duff is distinguished from the litter layer in that it has undergone sufficient decomposition so that the parent material is unidentifiable. Large piles of CWD and FWD created by windthrow, landslides, fires, and human activities such as harvesting are categorized as slash (U.S. Department of Agriculture Forest Service 2005).

Alabama currently has the fourth lowest DWM average of 11 Southern States. The State's forests have an average of 11.7 tons of DWM per acre, one-third less than the Southwide average of 17.7 tons per acre. Alabama ranks as either the third or fourth lowest State for CWD (1.2 tons per acre), FWD (2.5 tons per acre), duff (4.1 tons per acre), and slash (0.33 tons per acre). Litter is the only category in which the statewide

Juvenile red fox on a forest edge. (photo by Ronald Laubenstein, U.S. Fish and Wildlife Service, Bugwood.org)

average is higher than the southern average. Litter averages 3.4 tons per acre in Alabama forests and averages 3.0 tons per acre across the 11 Southern States (table 7).

Ozone

Ozone (O_3) is a naturally occurring compound that, when present in the upper atmosphere, helps protect the Earth's surface from ultraviolet rays. However, ozone is considered a pollutant in the lower atmosphere. Elevated exposures are an air quality problem that has the potential to affect human health, as well as forest ecosystem health and productivity over vast areas (Stolte 2001). Ozone damage monitoring in Alabama began with the establishment of a special ozone grid of 25 biomonitoring sites in 2002. The number of plots increased to 35 in 2003 as the grid was intensified. The goal has been to revisit these sites every year. This is not always done, as some sites are not visited due to logistics problems or failure to meet plot requirements. Ozone biomonitoring

sites are not located on either FIA or FHM plots because specific site and plant species requirements are mandatory for the ozone studies. The plots must contain at least 30 individuals of at least 2 and preferably 3 bioindicator species used to detect ozone injury (U.S. Department of Agriculture Forest Service 2005). The plants are then checked for ozone foliar symptoms.

Of the States monitored in the study, Alabama ranked second lowest in terms of percentage of plots with evidence of ozone damage. Florida was the only State to rank lower than Alabama, with injury symptoms in only 1.2 percent of plots. Alabama's average of 2.3 percent was far below the southern score of 20.6 percent. In 2005, only three sampled plots had any evidence of foliar injury. None of the Alabama biomonitoring sites sampled between 2001 and 2004 had any evidence of ozone damage. Future surveys will reveal whether this spike is a one-time aberration or the beginning of a trend (table 8).

Table 7—Average tons per acre of coarse woody debris, fine woody debris, duff, litter, slash and total down woody material by State, 2001 to 2005

State	Plots n	CWD	FWD	Duff	Litter	Slash	Total DWM
		- - - - - - - - - - - - - - - - *tons per acre* - - - - - - - - - - - - - - -					
Alabama	239	1.2	2.5	4.1	3.4	0.3	11.7
Arkansas	149	1.7	3.5	3.3	2.0	0.5	10.6
Florida	114	0.7	2.0	12.4	3.0	1.8	27.1
Georgia	241	1.4	2.7	6.7	3.2	1.6	15.8
Kentucky	133	2.3	3.7	4.9	2.1	0.0	13.3
Louisiana	101	1.3	2.0	4.3	2.3	0.1	10.5
North Carolina	183	2.4	3.1	12.3	4.7	0.1	40.6
South Carolina	136	1.5	3.2	9.7	4.4	0.5	19.3
Tennessee	160	2.5	2.9	7.7	3.4	9.7	26.4
Texas	357	1.0	1.9	3.1	1.9	1.1	8.9
Virginia	161	2.9	3.5	9.9	3.5	1.1	21.1
Total	1,974	1.6	2.7	6.6	3.0	1.5	17.7

CWD = coarse woody debris; FWD = fine woody debris; DWM = down woody material.
0.0 = a value of > 0.0 but < 0.05 for the cell.

A stream's edge. (photo by Andrew J. Hartsell)

Table 8—Total number of biomonitoring sites and number of sites with evidence of ozone foliar injury, by State and survey year

	Year										
	2001		2002		2003		2004		2005		
State	Bio-sites	Sites with injury	Bio-sites	Sites with injury	Bio-sites	Sites with injury	Bio-sites	Sites with injury	Bio-sites	Sites with injury	All sites with injury
	number										percent
Alabama	—	—	25	0	35	0	33	0	35	3	2.3
Arkansas	31	3	25	0	25	4	24	6	24	0	10.1
Florida	—	—	18	1	22	0	23	0	23	0	1.2
Georgia	30	7	45	15	48	19	47	10	48	13	29.4
Kentucky	16	10	31	10	31	18	25	9	38	3	35.5
Louisiana	22	7	21	0	21	0	24	0	20	0	6.5
North Carolina	37	17	42	10	31	14	47	10	49	6	27.7
South Carolina	26	9	29	14	39	20	31	16	26	14	48.3
Tennessee	56	12	38	7	40	13	41	5	40	4	19.0
Texas	—	—	17	3	18	1	29	0	26	0	4.4
Virginia	30	11	24	1	32	8	39	5	39	0	15.2
Total	248	76	316	61	342	97	363	61	368	43	20.7

— = no sample for the cell.

The forest products industry in Alabama is very diverse, ranging from small to medium-sized mills in all product categories to the very large softwood sawmills and pulpmills scattered all over the State. Alabama's forest products industry is a vital component of the State's economy. According to IMpact Analysis for PLANning (Abt 2002), a model generated by the Forest Service, the total economic importance of Alabama's forests in 2001 was calculated to be nearly $18.6 billion. The $18.6 billion includes all activities associated with the forest products industry and includes direct, indirect, and induced effects resulting from the industry operation.

In 2005, about 145 sawmills, pulpwood mills, and other primary wood-processing plants distributed across the State (fig. 22) directly employed > 33,289 individuals, with an annual payroll of nearly $1.33 billion. In 2005, the total value of shipments in Alabama's wood products and paper manufacturing sectors was > $11.51 billion (U.S. Department of Commerce 2005). Table 9 shows employment, payroll, and value of shipments for Alabama for the years 2000 through 2005. The number of employees fluctuated from > 40,600 in 2000 to the current number of 33,289 and averaged 34,843 employees over the 2000 to 2005 period. Over the same period, the payroll averaged $1.32 billion per year, reaching a peak of $1.4 billion in 2000. Value of shipments has remained relatively stable over the last 6 years and averaged > $10.1 billion per year for the time period.

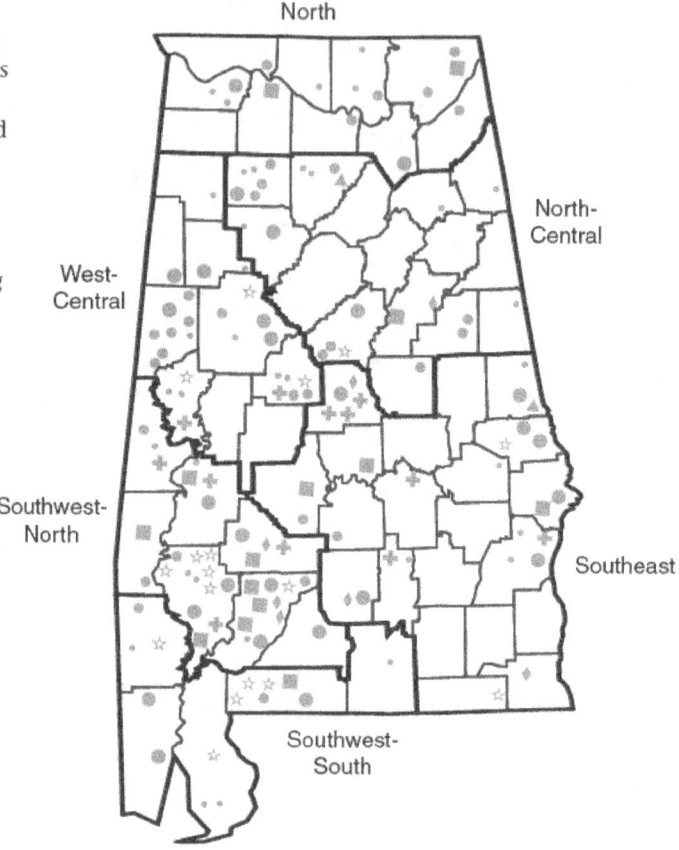

Primary wood-using mills

- Sawmill (< 5 mmbf)
- Sawmill (5–20 mmbf)
- Sawmill (> 20 mmbf)
- Composite panel
- Veneer
- Pulpmill
- Plywood mill
- Other mill

Figure 22—Primary wood-using mills by region, Alabama, 2005.

Table 9—U.S. Census Bureau statistics for the wood product and paper manufacturing industry groups, Alabama, 2000 to 2005

Year	Employees	Payroll	Value of shipments
	number	- - - thousand dollars - - -	
2000	40,620	1,404,634	10,324,234
2001	37,382	1,316,302	9,798,849
2002	34,318	1,322,725	9,397,532
2003	31,739	1,259,638	9,041,291
2004	31,709	1,289,640	10,794,038
2005	33,289	1,334,788	11,514,902

Timber Product Output and Removals

This section presents estimates of average annual roundwood product output and timber removals for the period 2000 through 2005. Estimates of timber product output (TPO) and plant residues were obtained from canvasses (questionnaires) sent to all primary wood-using mills in the State. The canvasses are used to determine the types and amount of roundwood, i.e., saw logs, pulpwood, poles, etc., received by each mill; the county of origin of the wood; the species used; and how the mills dispose of the bark and wood residues produced. The canvasses are conducted every 2 years by personnel from SRS and AFC. These data are used to augment FIA's annual inventory of timber removals by providing the product proportions for that segment of removals that is used for products. Individual studies are necessary to track trends and changes in product output levels. Industry surveys conducted in 2003 and 2005 were used to determine average annual product output for roundwood and plant byproducts (Bentley 2006). Total product output, averaged over the survey period, is the sum of the volume of roundwood products from all sources (growing stock and other sources) and the volume of plant byproducts, or the mill residues.

Total output of timber products, which includes domestic fuelwood and plant byproducts, averaged > 1.3 billion cubic feet per year between 2000 and 2005. Eighty-six percent, or 1.1 billion cubic feet, of the total output was from roundwood products, while the remainder was from plant byproducts (mill residue). Softwood species provided 76 percent (1.0 billion cubic feet) of the total product output volume. Hardwoods provided the remaining 24 percent (316 million cubic feet) of total output.

Alabama mills produced more pulpwood than any other wood product. Pulpwood production totaled nearly 681 million cubic feet in 2005, accounting for 51 percent of total product output for the State. Softwood pulpwood production totaled 479 million cubic feet, or 70 percent of total pulpwood production, while hardwood pulpwood production amounted to 202 million cubic feet. Plant byproducts, or mill residue, accounted for 25 and 8 percent, respectively, of total softwood and hardwood pulpwood production. The 133 million cubic feet of plant byproducts used for pulpwood production accounted for 71 percent of mill residue utilized for products other than industrial fuelwood. Saw-log production, used mainly for dimension lumber, totaled nearly 416 million cubic feet. Saw-log output accounted for 31 percent of the total TPO volume between 2000 and 2005. Veneer-log production totaled 103 million cubic feet, while composite panel production amounted to 48 million cubic feet. Veneer and composite panel production combined accounted for 11 percent of the total product output. Other industrial products, which include posts and poles, accounted for 50 million cubic feet, or nearly 4 percent, of total product output. Industrial products accounted for 98 percent of the State's total product output. Domestic fuelwood totaled > 27 million cubic feet, or 2 percent of total product output for the State. Mill residue used for industrial fuel amounted to 234 million cubic feet, or 56 percent of the utilized mill byproducts produced.

Figure 23 shows trends in average annual roundwood product output from 1963 through 2005. With the exception of roundwood used for other industrial products, which includes composite panel production, roundwood used for most industrial products and domestic fuelwood were down from the previous survey period. Average annual output of roundwood products (including domestic fuelwood) was down 8 percent, or 104 million cubic feet, to an average of 1.14 billion cubic feet between 2000 and 2005. Softwood roundwood production declined 6 percent to 840 million cubic feet, while hardwood roundwood production was down 14 percent to 297 million cubic feet. Roundwood saw-log and pulpwood production amounted to 414 and 547 million cubic feet, respectively. These two products accounted for nearly 85 percent of the total roundwood production for the State. Ninety percent of the roundwood products volume came from growing-stock trees, split between sawtimber (69 percent) and poletimber (31 percent) trees.

Other sources, which include cull trees, salvable dead trees, and stumps and tops of harvested trees, amounted to 112 million cubic feet.

Total timber removals, averaged over the time period, are the sum of the volume of roundwood products, logging residues (unused portions of trees left in the woods, which includes volume from tops, limbs, and stumps), and other removals (removals attributed to land clearing or land use changes) from growing-stock and nongrowing-stock sources. Removals from all sources, for both softwoods and hardwoods combined, totaled 1.6 billion cubic feet. Softwoods accounted for 66 percent of total removals. Volume used for roundwood products totaled 1.14 billion cubic feet, or 70 percent, of total removals. Logging residues and other removals amounted to 377.6 million cubic feet (23 percent) and 119.7 million cubic feet (7 percent) of total removals, respectively.

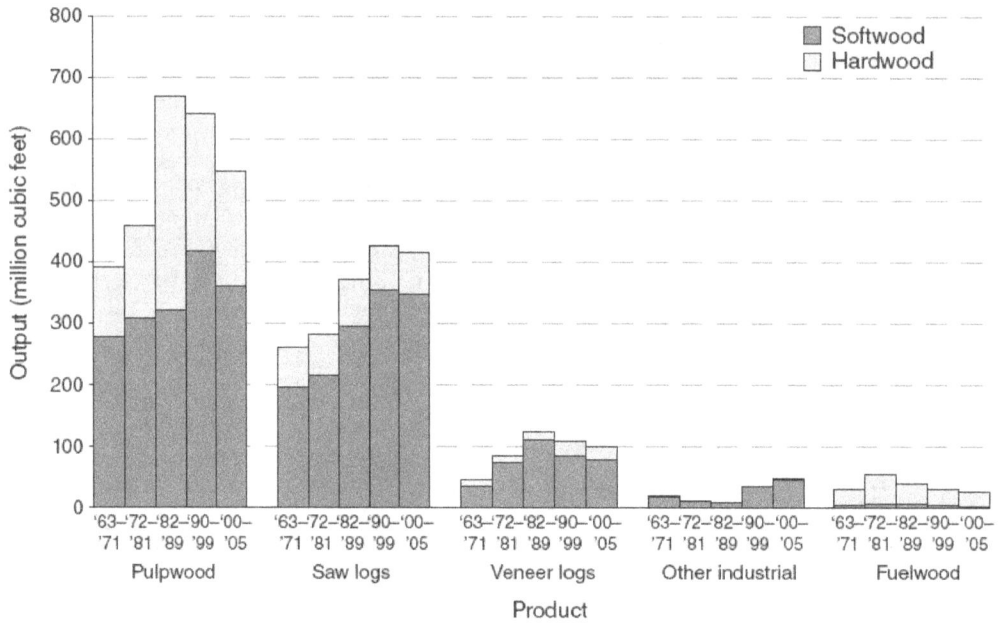

Figure 23—Average annual output of roundwood timber products by survey period, product, and species group, Alabama.

Specialty Forest Products

Nontimber benefits of the forest such as specialty forest products, recreation, water, wildlife habitat, and esthetic values also contribute greatly to the State's economy and the well-being of the State's general population. Specialty forest products or nontimber forest products (NTFP) have been harvested from Alabama's forests for many years. Although these products contribute a much smaller percentage to the overall economy than traditional forest products they are, none the less, very important and provide millions of dollars to many local rural economies each year. Many of these products are collected with very little forest disturbance and range from edible products (fruits, nuts, mushrooms, ramps, and maple syrup), to medicinal type products (saw palmetto and bloodroot), to floral and decorative products (galax,

pine tips for garlands, and grapevines), landscape products (pine straw and native plants), and specialty woods (burl and crotch wood for fine crafts).

According to a survey of county extension agents, as of April 2003, Alabama had a total of 1,411 NTFP enterprises (Chamberlain 2003). Table 10 shows the total number of NTFP enterprises Southwide. Fifty-three percent, or 754 of the NTFP enterprises, in the State, fell into the specialty wood and landscape categories. The medicinal plants and edible products comprised 279, or 20 percent, of the NTFP enterprises; while the floral and decorative products category had 378, or 27 percent, of the firms. Alabama ranked seventh in total number of NTFP enterprises in the southern region, accounting for 6 percent of the total NTFP firms.

Table 10—Distribution and total number of NTFP enterprises in the Southern United States as perceived by county extension agents

State	Edible	Specialty wood	Floral and decorative	Landscape	Medicinal	Total
			number			
Alabama	221	377	378	377	58	1,411
Arkansas	224	257	208	120	251	1,060
Florida	216	127	182	837	50	1,412
Georgia	250	186	384	1,086	68	1,974
Kentucky	490	826	562	373	2,670	4,921
Louisiana	249	119	94	81	8	551
Mississippi	234	252	207	192	15	900
North Carolina	526	452	3,283	1,326	770	6,357
Oklahoma	275	148	75	65	14	577
South Carolina	89	81	145	216	25	556
Tennessee	390	794	481	593	314	2,572
Texas	438	210	200	196	27	1,071
Virginia	239	370	698	376	262	1,945
Total	3,841	4,199	6,897	5,838	4,532	25,307

NTFP = nontimber forest products.

Abt, K.L.; Winter, S.A.; Huggett, R.J., Jr. 2002. Local economic impacts of forests. In: Wear, D.N.; Greis, J.G., eds. Southern forest resource assessment. Gen. Tech. Rep. SRS–53. Asheville, NC: U.S. Department of Agriculture Forest Service, Southern Research Station: 239–267.

Bentley, J.W.; Cartwright, W.E. 2006. Alabama's timber industry—an assessment of timber product output and use, 2003. Resour. Bull. SRS–107. Asheville, NC: U.S. Department of Agriculture Forest Service, Southern Research Station. 45 p.

Butler, B.J.; Leatherberry, E.C.; Williams, M.S. 2005. Design, implementation, and analysis methods for the national woodland owner survey. Gen. Tech. Rep. NE–336. Newtown Square, PA: U.S. Department of Agriculture Forest Service, Northeastern Research Station. 43 p.

Chamberlain, J.L.; Predny, M. 2003. Non-timber forest products enterprises in the South: perceived distribution and implications for sustainable forest management. In: Miller, J.E.; Midtbo, J.M., eds. Proceedings of the first national symposium on sustainable natural resource-based alternative enterprises. Mississippi State, MS: Mississippi State University Extension Service and Mississippi State University, Department of Wildlife and Fisheries: 48–63.

Duerr, W.A. 1946. Basic data on forest area and timber volumes from the southern forest survey, 1932-1936. For. Surv. Release 54. New Orleans: U.S. Department of Agriculture Forest Service, Southern Forest Experiment Station. 26 p.

Hartsell, A.J. 2009. Alabama's forests, 2000. Resour. Bull. SRS–143. Asheville, NC: U.S. Department of Agriculture Forest Service, Southern Research Station. 49 p.

Little, E.L., Jr. 1979. Checklist of United States trees (native and naturalized). Agric. Handb. 541. Washington, DC: U.S. Department of Agriculture. 375 p.

McWilliams, W.H. 1992. Forest resources of Alabama. Resour. Bull. SO–170. New Orleans: U.S. Department of Agriculture Forest Service, Southern Forest Experiment Station. 71 p.

Murphy, P.A. 1973. Alabama forests: trends and prospects. Resour. Bull. SO–42. New Orleans: U.S. Department of Agriculture Forest Service, Southern Forest Experiment Station. 36 p.

Rudis, V.A.; Rosson, J.F., Jr.; Kelly, J.F. 1984. Forest resources of Alabama. Resour. Bull. SO–98. New Orleans: U.S. Department of Agriculture Forest Service, Southern Forest Experiment Station. 55 p.

Smith, W.B.; Miles, P.D.; Vissage, J.S.; Pugh, S.A. 2004. Forest resources of the United States, 2002. Gen. Tech. Rep. NC–241. St. Paul, MN: U.S. Department of Agriculture Forest Service, North Central Research Station. 137 p.

Sternitzke, H.S. 1963. Alabama forests. Resour. Bull. SO–3. New Orleans: U.S. Department of Agriculture Forest Service, Southern Forest Experiment Station. 32 p.

Stolte, K.W. 2001. Forest health monitoring and forest inventory analysis programs monitor climate change effects in forest ecosystems. Human and Ecological Risk Assessment. 7(5): 1297–1316.

U.S. Department of Agriculture Forest Service. 2005. Forest inventory and analysis: Southern Research Station field guide. Field data collection procedures for phase 2 plots. Version 3.0. Knoxville, TN. 248 p. Vol. 1. http://www.srs.fs.fed.us/fia/data_acquisition/field_guide/FieldGuide.htm. [Date accessed: June 6, 2007].

U.S. Department of Commerce, Bureau of the Census. 2005. Statistics for the United States and States by industry group; 2005 and earlier years. Washington, DC: U.S. Government Printing Office. 52 p.

Wheeler, P.R. 1953. Forest statistics for Alabama. For. Surv. Release 73. New Orleans: U.S. Department of Agriculture Forest Service, Southern Forest Experiment Station. 52 p.

Alabama lies on the eastern edge of the Mississippi flyway, a major migration route for waterfowl such as these mallard ducks. (photo by Andrew J. Hartsell)

Afforestation. Area of land previously classified as nonforest that is converted to forest by planting trees or by natural reversion to forest.

Average annual mortality. Average annual volume of trees ≥ 5.0 inches d.b.h. that died from natural causes during the intersurvey period.

Average annual removals. Average annual volume of trees ≥ 5.0 inches d.b.h. removed from the inventory by harvesting, cultural operations (such as timber stand improvement), land clearing, or changes in land use during the intersurvey period.

Average net annual growth. Average annual net change in volume of trees ≥ 5.0 inches d.b.h. in the absence of cutting (gross growth minus mortality) during the intersurvey period.

Basal area. The area in square feet of the cross section at breast height of a single tree or of all the trees in a stand, usually expressed in square feet per acre.

Biomass. The aboveground fresh weight of solid wood and bark in live trees ≥ 1.0 inch d.b.h. from the ground to the tip of the tree. All foliage is excluded. The weight of wood and bark in lateral limbs, secondary limbs, and twigs < 0.5 inch in diameter at the point of occurrence on sapling-size trees is included but is excluded on poletimber and sawtimber-size trees.

Bole. That portion of a tree between a 1-foot stump and a 4-inch top d.o.b. in trees ≥ 5.0 inches d.b.h.

Census water. Streams, sloughs, estuaries, canals, and other moving bodies of water ≥ 200 feet wide, and lakes, reservoirs, ponds, and other permanent bodies of water ≥ 4.5 acres in area.

Commercial species. Tree species currently or potentially suitable for industrial wood products.

Composite panels. Roundwood products manufactured into chips, wafers, strands, flakes, shavings, or sawdust and then reconstituted into a variety of panel and engineered lumber products.

CRP. The Conservation Reserve Program, a major Federal afforestation program authorized by the 1985 Farm Bill.

D.b.h. Tree diameter in inches (outside bark) at breast height (4.5 feet aboveground).

Diameter class. A classification of trees based on tree d.b.h. Two-inch diameter classes are commonly used by Forest Inventory and Analysis, with the even inch as the approximate midpoint for a class. For example, the 6-inch class includes trees 5.0 through 6.9 inches d.b.h.

D.o.b. (diameter outside bark). Stem diameter including bark.

Down woody material. Woody pieces of trees and shrubs that have been uprooted (no longer supporting growth) or severed from their root system, not self-supporting, and are lying on the ground. Previously named down woody debris.

Forest land. Land at least 10 percent stocked by forest trees of any size, or formerly having had such tree cover, and not currently developed for nonforest use. The minimum area considered for classification is 1 acre. Forested strips must be at least 120 feet wide.

Forest management type. A classification of timberland based on forest type and stand origin.

Pine plantation. Stands that (1) have been artificially regenerated by planting or direct seeding, (2) are classed as a pine or other softwood forest type, and (3) have at least 10 percent stocking.

Natural pine. Stands that (1) have not been artificially regenerated, (2) are classed as a pine or other softwood forest type, and (3) have at least 10 percent stocking.

Oak-pine. Stands that have at least 10 percent stocking and classed as a forest type of oak-pine.

Upland hardwood. Stands that have at least 10 percent stocking and classed as an oak-hickory or maple-beech-birch forest type.

Lowland hardwood. Stands that have at least 10 percent stocking with a forest type of oak-gum-cypress, elm-ash-cottonwood, palm, or other tropical.

Nonstocked stands. Stands <10 percent stocked with live trees.

Forest type. A classification of forest land based on the species forming a plurality of live-tree stocking. Major eastern forest-type groups are:

White-red-jack pine. Forests in which eastern white pine, red pine, or jack pine, singly or in combination, constitute a plurality of the stocking. (Common associates include hemlock, birch, and maple.)

Spruce-fir. Forests in which spruce or true firs, singly or in combination, constitute a plurality of the stocking. (Common associates include maple, birch, and hemlock.)

Longleaf-slash pine. Forests in which longleaf or slash pine, singly or in combination, constitute a plurality of the stocking. (Common associates include oak, hickory, and gum.)

Loblolly-shortleaf pine. Forests in which loblolly pine, shortleaf pine, or other southern yellow pines, except longleaf or slash pine, singly or in combination, constitute a plurality of the stocking. (Common associates include oak, hickory, and gum.)

Oak-pine. Forests in which hardwoods (usually upland oaks) constitute a plurality of the stocking but in which pines account for 25 to 50 percent of the stocking. (Common associates include gum, hickory, and yellow-poplar.)

Oak-hickory. Forests in which upland oaks or hickory, singly or in combination, constitute a plurality of the stocking, except where pines account for 25 to 50 percent, in which case the stand would be classified oak-pine. (Common associates include yellow-poplar, elm, maple, and black walnut.)

Oak-gum-cypress. Bottomland forests in which tupelo, blackgum, sweetgum, oaks, or southern cypress, singly or in combination, constitute a plurality of the stocking, except where pines account for 25 to 50 percent, in which case the stand would be classified oak-pine. (Common associates include cottonwood, willow, ash, elm, hackberry, and maple.)

Elm-ash-cottonwood. Forests in which elm, ash, or cottonwood, singly or in combination, constitute a plurality of the stocking. (Common associates include willow, sycamore, beech, and maple.)

Maple-beech-birch. Forests in which maple, beech, or yellow birch, singly or in combination, constitute a plurality of the stocking. (Common associates include hemlock, elm, basswood, and white pine.)

Nonstocked stands. Stands < 10 percent stocked with live trees.

Forested tract size. The area of forest within the contiguous tract containing each Forest Inventory and Analysis sample plot.

Fresh weight. Mass of tree component at time of cutting.

Fuelwood. Roundwood harvested to produce some form of energy, e.g., heat and steam, in residential, industrial, or institutional settings.

Gross growth. Annual increase in volume of trees ≥ 5.0 inches d.b.h. in the absence of cutting and mortality. (Gross growth includes survivor growth, ingrowth, growth on ingrowth, growth on removals before removal, and growth on mortality before death.)

Growing-stock trees. Living trees of commercial species classified as sawtimber, poletimber, saplings, and seedlings. Trees must contain at least one 12-foot or two 8-foot logs in the saw-log portion, currently or potentially (if too small to qualify), to be classed as growing stock. The log(s) must meet dimension and merchantability standards to qualify. Trees must also have, currently or potentially, one-third of the gross board-foot volume in sound wood.

Growing-stock volume. The cubic-foot volume of sound wood in growing-stock trees at least 5.0 inches d.b.h. from a 1-foot stump to a minimum 4.0-inch top d.o.b. of the central stem.

Hardwoods. Dicotyledonous trees, usually broadleaf and deciduous.

> *Soft hardwoods.* Hardwood species with an average specific gravity of ≤ 0.50, such as gums, yellow-poplar, cottonwoods, red maple, basswoods, and willows.

> *Hard hardwoods.* Hardwood species with an average specific gravity > 0.50 such as oaks, hard maples, hickories, and beech.

Industrial wood. All roundwood products except fuelwood.

Land area. The area of dry land and land temporarily or partly covered by water, such as marshes, swamps, and river floodplains (omitting tidal flats below mean high tide), streams, sloughs, estuaries, and canals < 200 feet wide, and lakes, reservoirs, and ponds < 4.5 acres in area.

Live trees. All living trees. All size classes, all tree classes, and both commercial and noncommercial species are included.

Log grade. A classification of logs based on external characteristics indicating quality or value.

Logging residues. The unused merchantable portion of growing-stock trees cut or destroyed during logging operations.

Net annual change. Increase or decrease in volume of live trees at least 5.0 inches d.b.h. Net annual change is equal to net annual growth minus average annual removals.

Noncommercial species. Tree species of typically small size, poor form, or inferior quality that normally do not develop into trees suitable for industrial wood products.

Nonforest land. Land that has never supported forests and land formerly forested where timber production is precluded by development for other uses.

Nonstocked stands. Stands < 10 percent stocked with live trees.

Other forest land. Forest land other than timberland and productive-reserved forest land. It includes available and reserved forest land which is incapable of producing annually 20 cubic feet per acre of industrial wood under natural conditions, because of adverse site conditions such as sterile soils, dry climate, poor drainage, high elevation, steepness, or rockiness.

Other removals. The growing-stock volume of trees removed from the inventory by cultural operations such as timber stand improvement, land clearing, and other changes in land use, resulting in the removal of the trees from timberland.

Ownership. The property owned by one ownership unit, including all parcels of land in the United States.

National forest land. Federal land that has been legally designated as national forests or purchase units, and other land under the administration of the Forest Service, including experimental areas and Bankhead-Jones Title III land.

Forest industry land. Land owned by companies or individuals operating primary wood-using plants.

Nonindustrial private forest land. Privately owned land excluding forest industry land.

   Corporate. Owned by corporations, including incorporated farm ownerships.

   Individual. All lands owned by individuals, including farm operators.

Other public. An ownership class that includes all public lands except national forests.

   Miscellaneous Federal land. Federal land other than national forests.

   State, county, and municipal land. Land owned by States, counties, and local public agencies or municipalities or land leased to these governmental units for ≥ 50 years.

Plant residues. Wood material generated in the production of timber products at primary manufacturing plants.

Coarse residues. Material, such as slabs, edgings, trim, veneer cores and ends, suitable for chipping.

Fine residues. Material, such as sawdust, shavings, and veneer chippings, not suitable for chipping.

Plant byproducts. Residues (coarse or fine) used in the manufacture of industrial products for consumer use, or as fuel.

Unused plant residues. Residues (coarse or fine) not used for any product, including fuel.

Poletimber-size trees. Softwoods 5.0 to 8.9 inches d.b.h. and hardwoods 5.0 to 10.9 inches d.b.h.

Primary wood-using plants. Industries receiving roundwood or chips from roundwood for the manufacture of products, such as veneer, pulp, and lumber.

Productive-reserved forest land. Forest land sufficiently productive to qualify as timberland but withdrawn from timber utilization through statute or administrative regulation.

Pulpwood. A roundwood product that will be reduced to individual wood fibers by chemical or mechanical means. The fibers are used to make a broad generic group of pulp products that includes paper products, as well as fiberboard, insulating board, and paperboard.

Reforestation. Area of land previously classified as forest that is regenerated by planting trees or natural regeneration.

Rotten trees. Live trees of commercial species not containing at least one 12-foot saw log, or two noncontiguous saw logs, each 8 feet or longer, now or prospectively, primarily because of rot or missing sections, and with less than one-third of the gross board-foot tree volume in sound material.

Rough trees. Live trees of commercial species not containing at least one 12-foot saw log, or two noncontiguous saw logs, each 8 feet or longer, now or prospectively, primarily because of roughness, poor form, splits, and cracks, and with less than one-third of the gross board-foot tree volume in sound material; and live trees of noncommercial species.

Roundwood (roundwood logs). Logs, bolts, or other round sections cut from trees for industrial or consumer uses.

Roundwood chipped. Any timber cut primarily for pulpwood, delivered to nonpulpmills, chipped, and then sold to pulpmills as residues, including chipped tops, jump sections, whole trees, and pulpwood sticks.

Roundwood products. Any primary product such as lumber, poles, pilings, pulp, or fuelwood that is produced from roundwood.

Salvable dead trees. Standing or downed dead trees that were formerly growing stock and considered merchantable. Trees must be at least 5.0 inches d.b.h. to qualify.

Saplings. Live trees 1.0 to 5.0 inches d.b.h.

Saw log. A log meeting minimum standards of diameter, length, and defect, including logs at least 8 feet long, sound and straight, with a minimum diameter inside bark for softwoods of 6 inches (8 inches for hardwoods).

Saw-log portion. The part of the bole of sawtimber trees between a 1-foot stump and the saw-log top.

Saw-log top. The point on the bole of sawtimber trees above which a conventional saw log cannot be produced. The minimum saw-log top is 7.0 inches d.o.b. for softwoods and 9.0 inches d.o.b. for hardwoods.

Sawtimber-size trees. Softwoods ≥ 9.0 inches d.b.h. and hardwoods ≥ 11.0 inches d.b.h.

Sawtimber volume. Growing-stock volume in the saw-log portion of sawtimber-size trees in board feet (International 1/4-inch rule).

Seedlings. Trees < 1.0 inch d.b.h. and > 1 foot tall for hardwoods, > 6 inches tall for softwood, and > 0.5 inch in diameter at ground level for longleaf pine.

Select red oaks. A group of several red oak species composed of cherrybark, Shumard, and northern red oaks. Other red oak species are included in the "other red oaks" group.

Select white oaks. A group of several white oak species composed of white, swamp chestnut, swamp white, chinkapin, Durand, and bur oaks. Other white oak species are included in the "other white oaks" group.

Site class. A classification of forest land in terms of potential capacity to grow crops of industrial wood based on fully stocked natural stands.

Softwoods. Coniferous trees, usually evergreen, having leaves that are needles or scalelike.

Yellow pines. Loblolly, longleaf, slash, pond, shortleaf, pitch, Virginia, sand, spruce, and Table Mountain pines.

Other softwoods. Cypress, eastern redcedar, white cedar, eastern white pine, eastern hemlock, spruce, and fir.

Stand age. The average age of dominant and codominant trees in the stand.

Stand origin. A classification of forest stands describing their means of origin.

Planted. Planted or artificially seeded.

Natural. No evidence of artificial regeneration.

Stand-size class. A classification of forest land based on the diameter class distribution of live trees in the stand.

Sawtimber stands. Stands at least 10 percent stocked with live trees, with one-half or more of total stocking in sawtimber and poletimber trees, and with sawtimber stocking at least equal to poletimber stocking.

Poletimber stands. Stands at least 10 percent stocked with live trees, of which one-half or more of total stocking is in poletimber and sawtimber trees, and with poletimber stocking exceeding that of sawtimber.

Sapling-seedling stands. Stands at least 10 percent stocked with live trees of which more than one-half of total stocking is saplings and seedlings.

Nonstocked stands. Stands < 10 percent stocked with live trees.

Stocking. The degree of occupancy of land by trees, measured by basal area or the number of trees in a stand and spacing in the stand, compared with a minimum standard, depending on tree size, required to fully utilize the growth potential of the land.

Density of trees and basal area per acre required for full stocking:

D.b.h. class	Trees per acre for full stocking	Basal area
inches		square feet per acre
Seedlings (<1 inch)	600	—
2	560	—
4	460	—
6	340	67
8	240	84
10	155	85
12	115	90
14	90	96
16	72	101
18	60	106
20	51	111

— = not applicable.

Timberland. Forest land capable of producing 20 cubic feet of industrial wood per acre per year and not withdrawn from timber utilization.

Timber products. Roundwood products and byproducts.

Tree. Woody plants having one erect perennial stem or trunk at least 3 inches d.b.h., a more or less definitely formed crown of foliage, and a height of at least 13 feet (at maturity).

Tree grade. A classification of the saw-log portion of sawtimber trees based on: (1) the grade of the butt log or (2) the ability to produce at least one 12-foot or two 8-foot logs in the upper section of the saw-log portion. Tree grade is an indicator of quality; grade 1 is the best quality.

Upper-stem portion. The part of the main stem or fork of sawtimber trees above the saw-log top to minimum top diameter 4.0 inches outside bark or to the point where the main stem or fork breaks into limbs.

Veneer log. A roundwood product either rotary cut, sliced, stamped, or sawn into a variety of veneer products such as plywood, finished panels, veneer sheets, or sheathing.

Volume of live trees. The cubic-foot volume of sound wood in live trees at least 5.0 inches d.b.h. from a 1-foot stump to a minimum 4.0-inch top d.o.b. of the central stem.

Volume of saw-log portion of sawtimber trees. The cubic-foot volume of sound wood in the saw-log portion of sawtimber trees. Volume is the net result after deductions for rot, sweep, and other defects that affect use for lumber.

Metric equivalents

1 acre = 4046.86 m^2 or 0.404686 ha
1 cubic foot = 0.028317 m^3
1 inch = 2.54 cm or 0.0254 m
Breast height = 1.4 m above the ground
1 square foot = 929.03 cm^2 or 0.0929 m^2
1 square foot basal area per acre = 0.229568 m^2/ha
1 pound = 0.454 kg
1 ton = 0.907 MT

Running white-tailed buck. (Scott Bauer, USDA Agricultural Research Service, Bugwood.org)

Species List[a]

Common name	Scientific name[b]	Common name	Scientific name[b]
Softwoods		**Hardwoods (continued)**	
Atlantic white-cedar	*Chamaecyparis thyoides* (L.) B.S.P.	Mockernut hickory	*C. tomentosa* (Poir.) Nutt.
Southern redcedar	*Juniperus silicicola* (Small) Bailey	Allegheny chinkapin	*C. pumila* Mill.
Eastern redcedar	*J. virginiana* L.	Southern catalpa	*Catalpa bignonioides* Walt.
Sand pine	*Pinus clausa* (Chapm. ex Englem.) Vasey ex Sarg.	Sugarberry	*Celtis laevigata* Willd.
		Hackberry	*C. occidentalis* L.
Shortleaf pine	*P. echinata* Mill.	Eastern redbud	*Cercis canadensis* L.
Slash pine	*P. elliottii* Engelm.	Camphortree	*Cinnamomum camphora* (L.) J.S. Presl
Spruce pine	*P. glabra* Walt.		
Longleaf pine	*P. palustris* Mill.	Flowering dogwood	*Cornus florida* L.
Pond pine	*P. serotina* Michx.	Smoketree	*Cotinus obovatus* Raf.
Loblolly pine	*P. taeda* L.	Cockspur hawthorn	*Crataegus crus-galli* L.
Virginia pine	*P. virginiana* Mill.	Downy hawthorn	*C. mollis* Schelle
Baldcypress	*Taxodium distichum* (L.) Rich.	Common persimmon	*Diospyros virginiana* L.
Pondcypress	*T. distichum* var. *nutans* (Ait.) Sweet	Russian-olive	*Elaeagnus angustifolia* L.
Eastern hemlock	*Tsuga canadensis* (L.) Carr.	American beech	*Fagus grandifolia* Ehrh.
Hardwoods		White ash	*Fraxinus americana* L.
Florida maple	*Acer barbatum* Michx.	Carolina ash	*F. caroliniana* Mill.
Chalk maple	*A. leucoderme* Small	Green ash	*F. pennsylvanica* Marsh.
Boxelder	*A. negundo* L.	Black ash	*F. nigra* Marsh.
Red maple	*A. rubrum* L.	Pumpkin ash	*F. profunda* (Bush) Bush
Silver maple	*A. saccharinum* L.	Waterlocust	*Gleditsia aquatica* Marsh.
Sugar maple	*A. saccharum* Marsh.	Honeylocust	*G. triacanthos* L.
Yellow buckeye	*A. octandra* Marsh.	Loblolly-bay	*Gordonia lasianthus* L. Ellis
Ailanthus	*Ailanthus altissima* (Mill.) Swingle	Kentucky coffeetree	*Gymnocladus dioicus* (L.) K. Koch
Mimosa/silk tree	*Albizia julibrissin* Durazzini	Carolina silverbell	*Halesia carolina* L.
Serviceberry	*Amelanchier* spp. Med.	American holly	*Ilex opaca* Ait.
Papaw	*Asimina triloba* (L.) Dunal	Butternut	*Juglans cinerea* L.
Yellow birch	*Betula alleghaniensis* Britton	Black walnut	*J. nigra* L.
Sweet birch	*B. lenta* L.	Sweetgum	*Liquidambar styraciflua* L.
River birch	*B. nigra* L.	Yellow-poplar	*Liriodendron tulipifera* L.
Chittamwood, Gum bumelia	*Bumelia lanuginosa* (Michx.) Pers.	Osage-orange	*Maclura pomifera* (Raf.) Schneid.
		Cucumbertree	*Magnolia acuminata* L.
American hornbeam, musclewood	*Carpinus caroliniana* Walt.	Southern magnolia	*M. grandiflora* L.
		Bigleaf magnolia	*M. macrophylla* Michx.
Water hickory	*Carya aquatica* (Michx. f.) Nutt.	Umbrella magnolia	*M. tripetala* L.
Southern shagbark hickory	*C. carolinae-septentrionalis* (Ashe) Engl. & Graebn.	Sweetbay	*M. virginiana* L.
		Apple	*Malus* spp. Mill.
		Southern crab apple	*M. angustifolia* (Ait.) Michx.
Bitternut hickory	*C. cordiformis* (Wangenh.) K. Koch	Chinaberry	*Melia azedarach* L.
Pignut hickory	*C. glabra* (Mill.) Sweet	White mulberry	*Morus alba* L.
Pecan	*C. illinoensis* (Wangenh.) K. Koch	Red mulberry	*M. rubra* L.
Shellbark hickory	*C. laciniosa* (Michx. f.) Loud.	Water tupelo	*Nyssa aquatica* L.
Nutmeg hickory	*C. myristiciformis* (Michx. f.) Nutt.	Ogeechee tupelo	*N. ogeche* Bartr. ex Marsh
Shagbark hickory	*C. ovata* (Mill.) K. Koch	Blackgum	*N. sylvatica* Marsh.
Red hickory	*C. glabra* var. *odorata* (Marsh.) Little	Swamp tupelo	*N. sylvatica* var. *biflora* (Walt.) Sarg.
		Eastern hophornbeam	*Ostrya virginiana* (Mill.) K. Koch
Sand hickory	*C. pallida* (Ashe) Engl. & Graebn.	Sourwood	*Oxydendrum arboreum* (L.) DC.
Black hickory	*C. texana* Buckl.		

continued

Species List[a] (continued)

Common name	Scientific name[b]	Common name	Scientific name[b]
Hardwoods (continued)		**Hardwoods (continued)**	
Royal Paulownia	*Paulownia tomentosa* (Thunb.) Sieb. & Zucc. ex Steud	Dwarf live oak	*Q. minima (*Sarg.) Small
		Chinkapin oak	*Q. muehlenbergii* Engelm.
Redbay	*Persea borbonia* (L.) Spreng.	Water oak	*Q. nigra* L.
Water-elm, planer tree	*Planera aquatica* J.F. Gmel.	Nuttall oak	*Q. nuttallii* Palmer
Sycamore	*Platanus occidentalis* L.	Pin oak	*Q. palustris* Muenchh.
Eastern cottonwood	*Populus deltoides* Bartr. ex Marsh.	Willow oak	*Q. phellos* L.
Swamp cottonwood	*P. heterophylla* L.	Chestnut oak	*Q. prinus* L.
American plum	*Prunus americana* Marsh.	Northern red oak	*Q. rubra* L.
Pin cherry	*P. pensylvanica* L. f.	Shumard oak	*Q. shumardii* Buckl.
Black cherry	*P. serotina* Ehrh.	Post oak	*Q. stellata* Wangenh.
Chokecherry	*P. virginiana* L.	Delta post oak	*Q. stellata* var. *paludosa* Sarg.
White oak	*Quercus* alba L.	Black oak	*Q. velutina* Lam.
Swamp white oak	*Q. bicolor* Willd.	Live oak	*Q. virginiana* Mill.
Scarlet oak	*Q. coccinea* Muenchh.	Black locust	*Robinia pseudoacacia* L.
Durand oak	*Q. durandii* Buckl.	Black willow	*Salix nigra* Marsh.
Southern red oak	*Q. falcata* Michx.	Chinese tallowtree	*Sapium sebiferum* (L.) Roxb.
Cherrybark oak	*Q. falcata* var. *pagodifolia* Ell.	Sassafras	*Sassafras albidum* (Nutt.) Nees
Bluejack oak	*Q. incana* Bartr.	American basswood	*Tilia americana* L.
Turkey oak	*Q. laevis* Walt.	Carolina basswood	*T. caroliniana* Mill.
Laurel oak	*Q. laurifolia* Michx.	White basswood	*T. heterophylla* Vent.
Overcup oak	*Q. lyrata* Walt.	Winged elm	*Ulmus alata* Michx.
Dwarf post oak	*Q. margarettiae* Ashe	American elm	*U. americana* L.
Blackjack oak	*Q. marilandica* Muenchh.	Slippery elm	*U. rubra* Muhl.
Swamp chestnut oak	*Q. michauxii* Nutt.	September elm	*U. serotina* Sarg.

[a] Common and scientific names of tree species ≥ 1.0 inch in d.b.h. occurring in the FIA sample.
[b] Little (1979).

Morning mist. (SRS photo)

Crimson pitcher plant. (photo by James Henderson, Gulf South Research Corporation, Bugwood.org)

Alabama: The Yellowhammer State

Capital City: Montgomery

Location: 32.354 N, 86.284 W

Origin of State's Name: The origin of the name "Alabama" remains somewhat questionable. The traditional story is that Alabama comes from the Creek Indian language meaning "tribal town." Other sources claim it is derived from the Choctaw Indian language, meaning "thicket-clearers" or "vegetation-gatherers."

Nickname: Yellowhammer State, Heart of Dixie, Lizard State

Population: 4,599,030 (2006 estimate)

Geology:
  Land Area: 50,750 square miles; 30th largest
  Highest Point: Cheaha Mountain; 2,407 feet
  Inland Water: 1,673 square miles
  Largest City: Birmingham
  Lowest Point: Gulf Coast; sea level
  Coastline: 53 miles

Border States: Florida, Georgia, Mississippi, Tennessee

Constitution: 22nd State

Statehood: December 14, 1819

Agriculture: Poultry and eggs, cattle, nursery stock, peanuts, cotton, vegetables, milk, soybeans.

Industry: Paper, lumber, and wood products; mining, rubber and plastic products; transportation equipment; apparel.

Natural Resources: Alabama boasts a long growing season, lots of rain, and a wide variety of soils as important natural resources. Timber is also a valuable resource, and its chief commercial trees are pine, oak, gum, and yellow-poplar. Coal, iron ore, limestone, bauxite, and white marble provide a broad range of mineral resources. Dams on the Tennessee, Tallapoosa, and Sipsey Rivers are important sources of hydropower.

Tree: Southern longleaf pine—Longleaf pine is distributed primarily in the lower two-thirds of the State. It may be distinguished by the needles which occur in bundles of threes and are about 12 inches long. The cones are about 7 inches long. The legislature first designated the State tree as the southern pine tree in 1949. Because there are so many kinds of pine trees, the Southern Longleaf Pine was specified as the State tree of Alabama by the legislature in 1997.

Bird: Yellowhammer—Adopted in 1927, the correct common name, according to the American Ornithologists Union, is the northern flicker. Other names used locally include flicker, yellow-shafted flicker, southern flicker, and common flicker. The northern flicker is found throughout Alabama and is present all the months of the year.

Flower: Camellia—In 1927 a bill was introduced in the Alabama legislature making the goldenrod the State flower. On August 26, 1959, the State flower was changed to the camellia. Ladies in Butler County preferred the camellia since the goldenrod is a wildflower. They called the goldenrod a weed. Because there are several types of camellia, in June 1999, the legislature designated the camellia, *Camellia japonica* L., as the official State flower of Alabama. On the same day Alabama also chose a State wildflower since the camellia is not a native plant.

Song: The words of Alabama, the State song, were written by Julia S. Tutwiler, a distinguished educator and humanitarian. It was first sung to an Austrian air, but in 1931, through the interest of the Alabama Federation of Music Clubs, the music written by Mrs. Edna Gockel Gussen, Birmingham, was adopted by the legislature as the official State song.

Flag: Crimson St. Andrew's cross on a white field, patterned after the Confederate battle flag, was adopted in 1895. The bars forming the cross must not be < 6 inches broad and must extend diagonally across the flag from side to side.

Seal: The Great Seal of Alabama was approved by the Alabama Senate and House in 1939. The seal prominently displays the words "Alabama Great Seal" in the outer circle. The inner circle of the seal features an outline of the State of Alabama showing the State's major rivers, as well as the adjacent States. Interestingly, this version of the seal had actually been used back in 1819 when Alabama first became a State.

Motto: "Audemus jura nostra defendere" has been translated as "We Dare Maintain Our Rights" or "We Dare Defend Our Rights."

Information courtesy of: http://www.archives.alabama.gov, http://www.statesymbolsusa.org/Lists/state_name_origins.html, http://www.50states.com/alabama.htm, http://www.netstate.com, http://www.fortdeposit.info/alabamaadvantages.htm